旅游职业技能发展双语系列教材
丛书主编 谢苏

国际酒店求职指南

孙 嫘 王志毅 主编

北京·旅游教育出版社

总 序

谢 苏

　　高职涉外旅游专业培养的人才对应的岗位国际化程度较高,专业技能与英语应用能力高度重叠,故英语(或其他外语)应用能力是其核心能力。因此这类专业教学目标要求学生不仅要掌握扎实的专业技能,还能以专业背景为依托将英语应用能力熟练地运用于行业中。

　　然而,这些专业毕业生就业时的最大障碍就是英语应用能力不足,这不仅成为个人职业生涯发展的重大瓶颈,同时也是这类专业在人才培养中的软肋。究其根本原因还是这类专业仍将英语列为公共课或基础课,而不是作为专业课程。在这种传统体系中,英语教学的内容和评估与专业教学分属不同教学系统。既然是公共英语,教学就要兼顾公共性,其教材选定、教学模式和考核方式都具有一定公共性。这样做的后果是专业英语应用能力训练空间很小,不能充分满足涉外型专业的能力要求。但要加大专业英语训练的单位时间,又会导致学生总学习时数增加,这一来不但增加学生负担,也是对有限学习资源的不合理配置与使用。基于此,我们认为在涉外旅游专业应以双语专业课来取代与行业职业能力培养相关性较小的公共英语课。这样做不仅使英语应用能力训练从时间上得以充分保证;还能更有针对性地利用教学资源,补充和完善专业英语课程体系,凸显涉外型专业课程特色。这样做正符合了高职涉外型专业人才培养的特点。

基于上述考虑，我们编写了这一套《旅游职业技能发展双语系列教材》。这套教材适用于高职旅游院系涉外性强的专业或课程教学，其特点是将旅游职业技术和技能训练与英语教学有机结合在一起。对这些专业的学生来说，英语应用能力是岗位能力中的核心部分，这套教材所涉及内容多与岗位日常工作相关，难度不大，模式化程度较高。

这套教材的意义还有以下几点：

1. 有利于有条件的相关院系科学整合利用教学资源，充分发挥资源优势，保证人才培养目标的实现。这种整合不是单纯地取消公共英语课，而是提供更多单位时间培养和发展了与专业结合的英语应用能力，也就是强化了英语应用能力的教学。

将英语应用能力与专业能力素质培养有效融合是一种理想方式，能从根本上改变目前专业英语课中实践技能边缘化、形式化的现象。很多高职院校开设了专业英语课，但是这些课程目前采用的教材多以与专业相关的阅读材料为主要内容，教学也以单词、语法讲解为主要方式，教材几乎就是专业教材的英文版。加之大多专业英语课的课程设计往往过分注重课程逻辑性而力求凸显内容全面性，从而更导致对岗位特征的忽略或淡化。这样一来，专业英语课程中的重点成为语法和阅读，应用实践技能训练边缘化。涉外旅游专业的特点是不但强调英语应用能力是专业技能一部分，而且专业操作技术内涵并不太深。所以涉外旅游专业也完全可以尝试将英语与专业课中应用能力重合的知识点、能力点进行整合，即用双语进行专业课程教学。

2. 更有利于落实高职培养应用型、复合型旅游人才的目标。我们理解所谓应用型、复合型人才就是具有职场某类职业基本操作实践能力，并具备较高的相关职业能力和提升空间的专业人才。实际上,不同职业对应用型人才的要求是不同的。国际旅游的发展要求我们培养的学生不仅掌握扎实的专业能力,还能以专业背景为依托将外语应用能力熟练地运用于行业中。

另一方面,语言技能的习得和其他技能习得一样需要一定密集度的输入和反复练习。部分专业课程能用双语进行,就在时间上为英语应用实践技能提供了保障,同时由于和专业技能实操结合密切,教学材料也因此形象生动,便于学生理解和实训。这样也有利于培养学生学习兴趣,使其自觉提高学习能力。

3. 有利于高职旅游教育师资队伍提升水平,从而促进高职旅游教育质量提升。双语教学对师资提出了更高要求,涉外型旅游专业因其国际化特色,在师资队伍建设中就必然更强调英语语言应用能力和跨文化交际能力。通过课程建设培养师资队伍一直是我国高职有特色的师资队伍建设方法。实际上用英语进行专业课程教学并非没有前人经验,以国际著名的瑞士酒店服务和管理的职业教育为例,其所有的专业课程教学实施都是用英语进行。唯其如此,该国的酒店服务和管理专业才保证了国际化水平,成为该国职业教育的国际品牌。涉外型旅游专业中开展专业课双语教学会更加有力促进高职旅游专业的师资建设。

这套教材的主创人员都是从事多年高职旅游教育人士,结合国际旅游业发展的新形势,率先在双语专业课程教学方面做了探索实践,这套双语教材是高职旅游专业部分课程教学双语化的成果之一。我们编写这套教材的基本理念就是:以课程整合的形式将英语教学纳入专业能力训练,能更好地针对不同专业岗位的岗位技能设定教学环境和内容,从而提高教学资源的使用能效。我们从实践中也深深感到:教学改革不只是教学方法的改革,课程体系不变,在教学方法方面做再大努力也是缘木求鱼。教学理念的创新应该在课程体系改革建构中得到体现,在课程体系改革中应该允许专业有差异性,而不应只强求一致性。

我们也诚恳希望专家和广大师生对这套教材的不足之处提出宝贵意见,这样才有利于我们更深入的实践探索,为高职旅游教育的高质量发展做更多切实的努力。

前言

21世纪,迅猛发展的酒店业在经济全球化、品牌国际化、竞争白热化的推动下,对国际化人才的需求愈演愈烈。这一方面使得我国高职旅游教育面临着新的挑战,另一方面,也为我国旅游人才的国际化发展提供了广阔的就业空间。在机遇和挑战面前,如何能利用流利的英语以及娴熟的求职技能提高自身在面试疆场上的竞争力,是目前众多高职旅游类专业毕业生的殷切希望。

毋庸置疑,高等职业教育在培养和输送合格的旅游应用型人才方面起着至关重要的作用。然而,高职学生薄弱的英语应用能力却成为国际化人才培养中的重大瓶颈,既不利于人才培养目标的实现,也不利于专业的蓬勃发展。因而,不少高职院校在近年来不断增加学生的语言学习课程,主要集中在基础英语和专业英语两大方面,希望能全方位地提升学生听说读写能力。虽然在英语教学的强化下,学生的英语应用能力普遍得到了提升,但这是否就意味着学生能顺利地跻身于国际化人才之列？非也。要成为国际化人才首先就必须通过国际酒店的面试关。这一点正是目前广大院校在日常教学中所严重忽视的。许多学生虽然掌握了流利的英语和扎实的专业技能,但由于缺乏外企求职面试的知识和技能,最终痛失良机。

　　为了帮助读者在激烈的求职竞争中脱颖而出,我们编写了这本《国际酒店求职指南》,这也是我国高职旅游专业第一本专门针对国际酒店求职面试能力培养的双语教材。需要指出的是,这里所讲的"国际酒店求职",既指毕业生在我国境内的著名国际化品牌酒店谋求工作,又指毕业生直接在境外酒店谋求工作(工作地点为国外)。将求职面试技能与英语应用能力、酒店专业技能相结合,并强调教学的趣味性、开放性、可操作性和可复制性是这本教材最大的特点。该教材的编写人员都是高职旅游类专业双师双语型教师,既具有丰富的国际酒店工作经验,又曾多次赴国外知名旅游企业和院校学习进修,同时还负责其所在院校与国际知名酒店集团的合作,长期承担着学生的海外职业生涯指导课程以及求职面试技能的培训工作。

　　由于英语是国际酒店业中最普遍的交际语言,因而该教材采用双语编写,相关理论和知识要点是以学习焦点的形式用汉语介绍,而对话、学以致用以及补充阅读均用英语编写(难点进行了注释)。该教材主要适用于酒店管理专业和涉外旅游专业,当然对于其他旅游类相关专业和涉外型专业学生的英文求职面试,也具有较强的指导作用。

　　目标:通过对本教材的学习,学生能了解并掌握获取求职信息的基本途径;能熟练准确地撰写英文求职材料;能正确得体地运用求职面试礼仪;能较流畅地与面试官用英语进行沟通;能把握涉外酒店不同岗位的需求特点进行自我展示和面试应对。

　　内容编排:本教材分为四个篇章,共10个单元。即求职准备篇(3个单元)、求职礼仪篇(2个单元)、面试应对篇(2个单元)以及职位实战篇(3个单元)。其中,职位实战篇是根据高职毕业生初入职场时最主要的求职岗位来进行分类介绍。

体例:每个单元大体由以下五大部分组成。

案例导入(Lead-in)由一则案例来导入该单元的学习焦点,启发学生的学习兴趣和思维。

学习焦点(Focus)介绍本单元应掌握的相关理论和知识要点。

英语情景对话(Dialogue)结合每一单元应掌握的相关理论和知识要点,以对话形式展开,不仅能帮助读者更好地理解掌握学习焦点,还多以开放式结尾,以启发读者发散性思维。

学以致用(Transference)围绕学习焦点的内容,通过形式多样的英语练习题目,强化训练学生熟练掌握本单元所介绍的面试技能,有利于当堂巩固。在训练中,我们也为每个单元安排了听力练习,旨在提升学生的听力能力和交流能力。

补充阅读(Reading)旨在以英语阅读的形式扩充与面试相关的背景知识,侧重训练学生准确阅读理解英文信息并对其做出相应处理的能力。

教学建议:由于本教材主要针对毕业生求职面试,故安排在高年级第四或第五学期为宜。建议学时为40~48。其中,求职准备篇建议学时8~10,教学重点为英文简历和求职信撰写;求职礼仪篇建议学时为6~8,教学重点为面试礼仪,侧重训练学生在面试时的走姿、站姿、坐姿、面部表情和肢体语言等;面试应对篇建议学时为8~10,教学重点为用英文讲述故事以及常规面试问题的应答策略;职位实战篇建议学时为18~20,教学重点为不同部门中不同岗位的求职面试技巧,这一篇也是整个教学中的重点所在。

实践性教学活动:教学实践是保证本教材教学实施达到预期效果的重要环节。在教学实施中,教师应注意至少将一半学时用来指导学生实践。尤其是在职位实战篇中,应大量运用模拟面试的形式,侧重训练学生在面试现场的沟通能力、抗压能力、应变能力和决策能力。如果有条件,还可邀请国内涉外酒店的专家来参与模拟面试,指导学生实践。

由于涉外酒店求职指导类课程的开设还处于实践探索阶段,我们希望得到广大同行们的支持和指教。该教材难免有谬误之处,诚恳希望得到大家指正。

(本书配有录音资料,若有需要,请与旅游教育出版社发行部联系)

编者

CONTENTS

求职准备篇

第一章 求职前的准备工作(Application Preparations) ········· 3
   案例导入(Lead-in) ········· 3
   1.1 学习焦点(Focus) ········· 3
   1.2 英语情景对话(Dialogue) ········· 13
   1.3 学以致用(Transference) ········· 17
   1.4 补充英语阅读(Reading) ········· 20

第二章 英文求职简历(Resume or Curriculum Vitae) ········· 23
   案例导入(Lead-in) ········· 23
   2.1 学习焦点(Focus) ········· 23
   2.2 英语情景对话(Dialogue) ········· 39
   2.3 学以致用(Transference) ········· 43
   2.4 补充英语阅读(Reading) ········· 45

第三章 英文求职信(Cover Letter) ········· 48
   案例导入(Lead-in) ········· 48
   3.1 学习焦点(Focus) ········· 48
   3.2 英语情景对话(Dialogue) ········· 64
   3.3 学以致用(Transference) ········· 67

3.4 补充英语阅读(Reading) ·· 71

求职礼仪篇

第四章 求职形象礼仪(Image and Good Manners) ················ 77
 案例导入(Lead-in) ··· 77
 4.1 学习焦点(Focus) ··· 77
 4.2 英语情景对话(Dialogues) ······································ 85
 4.3 学以致用(Transference) ·· 88
 4.4 补充英语阅读(Reading) ·· 91

第五章 面试礼仪(Job Interview Etiquette) ··························· 94
 案例导入(Lead-in) ··· 94
 5.1 学习焦点(Focus) ··· 94
 5.2 英语情景对话(Dialogues) ······································ 100
 5.3 学以致用(Transference) ·· 103
 5.4 补充英语阅读(Reading) ·· 105

面试应对篇

第六章 如何包装自我(How to Set up Good Self-image) ········· 111
 案例导入(Lead-in) ··· 111
 6.1 学习焦点(Focus) ··· 111
 6.2 英语情景对话(Dialogues) ······································ 120
 6.3 学以致用(Transference) ·· 123
 6.4 补充英语阅读(Reading) ·· 126

第七章 如何应对面试中的问题
  (How to Handle the Questions for Interview) ············ 129
 案例导入(Lead-in) ··· 129
 7.1 学习焦点(Focus) ··· 129
 7.2 英语情景对话(Dialogues) ······································ 138

  7.3 学以致用(Transference) ········· 141

  7.4 补充英语阅读(Reading) ········· 146

职位实战篇

第八章 申请前厅部工作人员(How to Apply for Jobs in Front Office) ······ 151

 案例导入(Lead-in) ········· 151

  8.1 学习焦点(Focus) ········· 151

  8.2 英语情景对话(Dialogues) ········· 156

  8.3 学以致用(Transference) ········· 160

  8.4 补充英语阅读(Reading) ········· 165

第九章 申请餐饮部工作人员
    (How to Apply for Jobs in Food and Beverage Department) ······ 168

 案例导入(Lead-in) ········· 168

  9.1 学习焦点(Focus) ········· 168

  9.2 英语情景对话(Dialogues) ········· 173

  9.3 学以致用(Transference) ········· 177

  9.4 补充英语阅读(Reading) ········· 181

第十章 申请客房部工作人员
    (How to Apply for Jobs in Housekeeping Department) ······ 184

 案例导入(Lead-in) ········· 184

  10.1 学习焦点(Focus) ········· 184

  10.2 英语情景对话(Dialogues) ········· 189

  10.3 学以致用(Transference) ········· 193

  10.4 补充英语阅读(Reading) ········· 198

附录 A ········· 201

附录 B ········· 203

参考文献 ········· 204

求职准备篇

第一章 求职前的准备工作（Application Preparations）

案例导入（Lead-in）

求职人：徐峰（某旅游院校酒店管理专业，现就职于某五星级国际知名大酒店）

临近毕业，徐峰和同学们一样都忙得团团乱转，哪里有大型服务行业招聘会，哪里就有他们的身影。短短一个月内，他向当地众多的高星级酒店投了简历。良好的开端是成功的一半。不久，各酒店的面试通知陆续传来。然而，徐峰的第一次面试却是失败的。在面试中，某酒店的人力资源部经理问了他三个有关该酒店产品、服务和经营理念的问题，他一个都没有回答上来，结果就被淘汰出局了。面对失败，徐峰进行了反思。他开始寻找应对面试的资料，并在每次面试之前详细地了解对方的基本情况。甚至在面试的前几天还专门到目标酒店进行考察，感受企业氛围，了解酒店相关产品和服务。在接下来的某五星级国际知名酒店的面试中，有备而来的徐峰凭着过硬的专业知识和灵敏的头脑，流利地回答了考官的问题，并对酒店客房销售谈出了自己的想法。最后，他顺利地得到了工作机会。

问题1　徐峰在第一次面试中失败的根本原因是什么？

问题2　徐峰最终又为什么会在面试中取得成功呢？

1.1 学习焦点（Focus）

知彼知己，百战不殆。在就业压力与日俱增的今天，社会经验不足的大学生们唯有做好充分的准备工作，方能在激烈的面试角逐中把握时机，崭露头角。那何谓准备充分呢？第一要了解自我，即进行合理的自我定位；第二要了解企业，那就需要获取求职信息来得以实现；第三要"量体裁衣"，也就是针对企业的需要，准备求职材料。本章主要围绕这三个方面来进行讨论。

1.1.1 自我定位

很多人都认为，找工作就是从投简历开始。事实上，简历投得成功与否在很大程度上是取决于是否进行了自我定位。一份理想的工作既应该是自己喜欢的，又应该是自己擅长的。但如果一个人连自己想做什么都不知道，连自己的优势劣势是什么都不清楚，那又何谈一份理想的工作呢？可见，自我定位才是求职过程中的第一个环节，也是至关重要的一个环节。通过自我定位，求职者可以明确自己想干什么、能干什么、应该干什么，以及就业期望值。而这些就是寻求一份理想工作的开始。

既然自我定位如此重要，那究竟应该如何来进行呢？我们将自我定位的途径归纳为三种：从过去行为中认知自我；从社会实践中验证自我；从实际事例中总结自我。

（1）从过去行为中认知自我。一个人过去的行为往往体现出自身的性格和喜好。作为面临择业的大学生们，其人格特征已基本成型，因此，通过分析自己过去的行为可以清楚地了解自我。在实际操作中，可以通过做几份比较权威的性格测试或者是职业测试来认知自我。当然，测试结果不一定反映的是一个全面的自我，但是这些测试不失为一种良好的工具，客观全面地了解一下自身的性格特点。在测试的基础上，再回顾过往的具体经历，尤其是影响力较大的，最好用笔纸将其列出来。例如，大学期间自己将主要精力放在了什么方面？自己对哪个领域的知识比较感兴趣？是否参加过社团活动或校级以上的大型活动？大学经历过的比较重大的事情是什么，当时自己所做出的选择又是怎样的？性格中有哪些优缺点？从哪些事例可以看出自己的优缺点？等等。通过回答这些问题，一方面可以梳理过往的经历，为撰写简历做好准备，另一方面则是通过过去的行为全面地认识自我。

（2）从社会实践中验证自我。实践出真知。要探索自身在未来职场中的发展道路，就必须要先了解职场生活，而实践就是最好的了解途径。由于大学生还未正式踏入社会,对社会的了解程度只是停留在表面,难以客观地、理性地把握职业方向。因而,对于自己是否适合这个职位、这个行业是否具有发展前景,一定要通过亲身经历才能验证。对于大学生而言,社会实践主要有两种途径,一是实习,二是兼职。相比兼职而言,实习更利于验证自我。这主要是因为实习工作的时间相对较长,对企业运作或者行业基本情况的了解也更为深入;另一方面实习招聘流程相对规范,可以在寻找实习机会的过程中积累面试经验。

(3)从实际事例中总结自我。对自我进行总结是自我定位中的必经阶段,与认知自我和验证自我一起形成了一个完整的自我探索过程。在此阶段,通常要回答自己三个问题。第一个问题:我最想要的是什么?是金钱,工作环境,还是社会地位,等等。这个问题其实就是关于自己的职业生涯目标与期望值。它往往会决定今后职业发展的大方向。作答时,应尽可能列出自己各个方面的答案,越详细越好。第二个问题:我最适合做什么?回答这个问题,一定要本着实事求是的态度,才能客观、科学地定位自己。首先,应将自己的优势列出来,如团队合作精神、学习创新能力、敬业精神、勤奋上进等,而且每一个优势都要有事例作为支撑。其次,就是将自认为或者他人提及的缺点列出来,如粗心、浮躁、口才欠佳、缺乏主动性,等等。当然,这些缺点也要有所依据,不能妄自菲薄。罗列缺点时顺便把改正缺点的方法也列出来。需要注意的是,像内向、不喜欢与人交往这类,属于性格特点,严格来说并不是缺点,但如果性格与喜欢从事的工作有冲突,则可以将此类性格特点视为缺点,并详列改正方法。第三个问题:我的兴趣点在哪里?这个问题实质上就是探讨自己喜欢什么样的工作。回答这个问题,首先要了解自己的兴趣爱好。当然,有些人会说,只要薪水高的工作我就会喜欢。但薪水的高低事实上是关乎工作的期望值,属于第一个问题的范畴。还有些人会认为兴趣会随着时间和年龄变化而变化,很难说清楚自己到底喜欢什么。因此,对于那些找不到自己兴趣点的人而言,可以尝试寻找工作中自己所不能容忍的事物。这样,通过排除法,基本上就可以了解到自己的兴趣点在哪里了。值得注意的是,以上所要求的事例是个人简历中的关键要素,也是面试过程中的有力例证,因而一定要花精力去充分准备,这样才能为自己的能力和实力做一个有力的证明。

1.1.2 求职信息的获取

毕业生求职择业,不仅取决于整个社会的政治、经济状况以及自身的能力素养,而且还取决于是否拥有大量的求职信息。所谓求职信息,就是指通过各种媒介传播的与求职相关的消息和情况。从广义上来讲,它不仅仅是具体用人单位的需求信息,还包括国家有关毕业生就业的方针、政策、法规,地方制定的有关就业政策,专业对口相关行业、企业在国民经济和社会发展中所处的地位、作用和发展势头等;从狭义来讲,它主要是指某一用人单位的性质、人员结构、经营状况、发展前景、工作环境、需求状况、任职要求,等等。对于面临求职择业的毕业生来说,在竞争白热化的人才市场中,能够及时、准确地了解、获取求职信息,并认真全面地对这些信息进行分析、筛选和整理,才是成功就业的基础。

1.1.2.1 求职信息的获取渠道

利用各种渠道掌握相关的求职信息,是获得理想工作的前提。下面,就针对几种常见的求职信息获取渠道进行介绍。

(1)各级、各类"双向选择"、"供需见面"会。这类活动有的是由一个学校或多校联合举办的,有的是一省或几省联办的,也有的是由地市县单独举办,组织毕业生和用人单位直接见面。由于参加招聘会的用人单位都是针对某些专业而来,招聘具有很强的目的性,因而求职信息的有效性也最高。有些毕业生甚至会在招聘会现场直接与用人单位签订就业协议。

(2)各高校的主管部门。高校的毕业生就业办公室(或指导中心),作为毕业生就业的重要中介机构,与中央有关部委和各省市的毕业生就业主管部门以及有关用人单位保持着密切的联系。学校的主管部门通常都有能及时掌握国家有关就业政策规定、地方的有关政策、各地举办"双选"活动的信息、有关用人单位简介材料以及需求信息等。无论是从数量上看还是从质量上看,高校的主管部门所提供的信息都具有明显的优势,因而是毕业生们获取就业信息的重要渠道。

(3)各级毕业就业主管部门和就业指导机构。每年教育部都要制定毕业生就业的有关方针、政策,各省、自治区、直辖市的主管部门也要相应地制定实施意见;国家教委和各地的毕业生就业指导机构,也要开展信息交流和咨询服务,这也是获取就业信息的重要渠道。

(4) 各类人才交流网站。当今社会已进入了信息化时代,网络求职、网络招聘已成为一种常见的求职方式。一般可通过政府管理部门网站、专业人才交流网站和目标行业或目标企业网站等多个途径搜索求职信息。目前,我国已有数百个人才交流网站。通过登录这些网站,人们可以了解到很多企业概况,找到相关的求职信息,查询有关的政策规定。

(5) 有关新闻媒介。毕业生就业作为社会普遍关注的热点问题,自然也是新闻媒介报道的焦点。很多企业,尤其是外资企业,会在报纸杂志上刊登招聘广告,对职位性质、求职者的条件、需要提供的材料、联系方式等事项进行说明。

(6) 各类社会关系。每位毕业生都会有自己的人际关系网,包括教师、家长、校友、亲朋好友等。他们分布在社会的各个领域,通过他们可以了解到比较准确的求职信息。一般而言,用人单位向社会发布招聘信息后,将会收到大量内容所差无几的求职材料。面对如此众多的陌生人,用人单位一时间也很难分辨出哪一个更为合适。但如果有亲朋好友为你推荐,那成功的机会就会更大一些。即便是在西方发达国家,也经常会有老员工推荐新员工,有的企业还会对积极推荐的员工予以奖励。可见,社会关系也是求职中不可忽略的一个因素。

(7) 利用社会实践、专业实习或业余兼职获取信息。大学生到用人单位参加社会实践和实习活动,不仅有利于开阔视野,学以致用,还可以获取用人单位的全面准确的人才需求信息。参加这些活动是大学生自我推销,赢得用人单位好感与信任的最佳机会。因此,大学生应充分利用寒暑假、业余时间开展社会实践或实习活动,适当做一些兼职、到各专业对口单位锻炼,体现自己的才华、能力、忠诚度与敬业精神,同时更了解就业形势、行业情况、职业发展机会、用人单位需求信息以及内部管理等,为日后的求职竞争奠定良好的基础。

(8) 直接与用人单位联系就业信息。这是一种毛遂自荐的方式,但比较冒险,因为某些用人单位并不喜欢被人打搅,所以采用这种方式一定要注意技巧。可以用自荐信的形式先与你认为适合的用人单位联系,待确定重要目标后,再通过电话来预约登门拜访的时间。如果遭到用人单位的回绝,切不可一意孤行,鲁莽造访。因为这样做只会给用人单位留下更糟的印象。

1.1.2.2 求职信息的筛选

并非所有搜集到的求职信息都是有用的。过多过泛的信息量往往会给人以错觉,影响判断力。因此,毕业生对于收集到的需求信息,应结合自我定位的实际情况,加以筛选处理,去粗取精、去伪存真,有目的、有针对性地进行排列、整理和分析,最终留存对自己择业有用的信息。筛选求职信息应注意以下几个方面:

(1)善于对比。通过多种途径获得的求职信息可能会显得杂乱无序,这就需要进行科学的排序。排序时,首先需要注意的是识辨真伪,剔除过时的、虚假的信息,其次就是将与自己的专业、兴趣、意愿等相关的信息提取出来。

(2)分清主次。把与自己有关的信息按重要程度依次排列,标明并注意留存。一般的信息仅供求职者参考,而对于重要信息,则要迅速做出反应,把握信息的时效性,争取主动权。

(3)深入了解。对于重要信息,毕业生要注意寻根究底,争取对该单位和职位有一个较为深入的认识。一方面要核实用人单位的性质、隶属关系、工作条件、发展前景、管理状况、地理环境等基本情况及有无新进员工、主管部门的人事规定、户口要求等;另一方面要查实用人单位对求职者的要求。详细掌握这些材料,有助于早日赢得面试的机会。

(4)人职匹配。在筛选信息的过程中,要把握一个重要的原则,即"适合自己的就是最好的",这一点应是筛选信息的核心。毕业生在筛选信息时,要结合自己的兴趣、爱好、能力等条件,再来决定自己能够适应和胜任的职业。切忌好高骛远、人云亦云、迷失自我。那些不顾自己的专长,仅以待遇、工作地点作为首选原则的毕业生们,即便侥幸在求职中暂时取得"成功",在未来的发展中也会逐渐暴露出自己的弱势,缺乏发展后劲。

1.1.3 求职材料的准备

在求职过程中,反映毕业生情况的书面材料通常是绝大部分用人单位安排面试的依据,也是毕业生自我推销的名片。用人单位往往通过这些书面材料来判断和评价毕业生的学习成绩、综合素质和工作潜力。因此,要想成功地向用人单位推销自己,准备具有说服力和吸引力的求职材料是毕业生迈向成功的第一步。

求职材料主要包括毕业生的个人简历、求职信、就业推荐表、成绩单以及其他能说明个人能力和业绩的证明材料,如学历证书、各类技能等级证书、已发表的文章、论文、取得的成果等。特别说明的是,由于本书主要讨论的是有关国际酒店求职和面试的内容,因此,上述求职材料除了准备中文之外,还必须要准备相应的英文版本。尤其是近年来,在旅游全球化背景下,我国酒店业的国际化已经成为必然的发展趋势。不少国际知名的酒店集团,在招聘员工时,明确提出求职人员所提供的求职材料必须是用英文撰写的。可见,英文求职材料对于那些想迈入外资企业甚至是境外企业的求职人士而言,的确是非常重要的。本书在第二章和第三章中会专门讨论英文求职简历和求职信的写作方法,在此仅对其他求职材料进行介绍。

(1)毕业生就业推荐表。该表是反映毕业生在校期间的综合情况并附有学校书面意见的推荐表。主要包括:毕业生基本资料、照片、学历、社会工作、获奖情况、科研情况、个人兴趣特长等,一般还应附有教务部门出具的成绩单。其中,该表的综合评定及推荐意见部分是由最了解毕业生全面情况的辅导员填写,并且是以组织负责的形式向用人单位推荐,具有较大的权威性和可靠性,所以大部分用人单位历来把该表作为接收毕业生的主要依据。下面是一份毕业生就业推荐表的样本,以供参考。

武汉职业技术学院毕业生就业推荐表

姓名	王××	性别	女	出生年月	1988-9	民族	汉	政治面貌	中共党员	健康状况	良好
专业	酒店管理(英语方向)				学制	三		第二专业		无	
外语水平		CET 四级			计算机能力			熟练(没有计算机等级证书的)			
原户口所在地		湖北 省			武汉 市			县(区)			
学生联系地址、邮编、电话		武汉市关山大道463号 武汉职业技术学院 东区学生宿舍2栋308室 430074 159×××××××									
社会工作情况	特长及担任职务	有良好的英语听说读写能力,还具有一定的日语基础; 熟练掌握酒店 Opera 操作系统以及计算机办公软件; 2009.7-2010.7 在北京建国大酒店前厅部实习,并获得优秀实习生的称号等。									

续表

奖惩情况	08-09年度校级综合奖学金一等奖 09-10年度校级综合奖学金一等奖 2009年5月获校级英语演讲比赛一等奖
推荐意见	该生在校期间表现良好,学习认真,有较强的专业实践能力。性格开朗,兴趣广泛,尊敬老师,关心集体,团结同学,积极参与校内外各项社会实践活动。 院(系)章 2010年10月30日
备注	

(2)实习证明书。绝大部分用人单位都希望前来求职的毕业生能具备一定的与专业相关的社会实践能力。因此,能证明自身社会经历和能力等情况的证书或证明人也是不可忽视的求职材料。对于立志工作于国际酒店的毕业生而言,应该将自己专业实习的相关证书准备好。如果证书是中文版的,还应该将中文版翻译成英文版作为附件。如有必要,还应与过去或现在的上司、老师联系,征得他们的同意,请他们为自己的工作表现和能力等作证。下面,提供一份酒店实习证明的样本以供参考。

(3)求职申请表。在面试前后,用人单位一般会要求求职人员填写求职申请表。了解求职申请表的填写方法是非常有必要的。因为人力资源部经理不但要看你的学历、经历和业绩,同时还要考察你如何用英文组织并表达它们的能力。下面,提供一份已填写好的求职申请表的英汉对照,以供学习。

第一章 求职前的准备工作(Application Preparations)

英文版:

EMPLOYMENT APPLICATION

No. 1

POSITION APPLIED: Receptionist

BASIC INFORMATION	FIRST NAME: Li LAST NAME: Wang	ENGLISH NAME: Catherine	
	PLACE OF BIRTH: Wuhan	HEIGHT(cm): 163	
	DATE OF BIRTH: July 1, 1989	WEIGHT(kg): 50	
	ID NUMBER: 420109198907011943	GENDER: Female	
	MOTHER NAME: Zhang Hong	MARITAL STATUS: Unmarried	
	FATHER NAME: Wang Gang	NATIONALITY: China	

	NAME OF SCHOOL / COLLEGE / UNIVERSITY	PERIOD		MAJOR
EDUCATION BACKGROUND		FROM Mth/Yr	TO Mth/Yr	
	Wuhan Technic College	09/2008	06/2010	Hotel Management

TRAINING BACKGROUND	Crowne Plaza Hotels & Resorts in Shenzhen	07/2009	09/2009	

Awards Received (if any):
Second Prize in English Speech Contest at Wuhan Technic College, 2010

Special SKILLS:
Excellent in English speaking and writing;
Expert at Office programs such as Word, Excel, PowerPoint;
Good at Swimming

	NAME OF COMPANY/HOTEL	PERIOD		POSITON
EMPLOYMENT RECORD		FROM Mth/Yr	TO Mth/Yr	
	Crowne Plaza Hotels & Resorts in Shenzhen	07/2009	07/2010	Receptionist

Job Description:
As a receptionist, I was responsible for checking guests in and out of the hotel and allocating rooms. I also operated the switchboard and made reservations for accommodation. I had to do cashiering and auditing, such as preparing the accounts for meetings and functions. I am a responsible and careful person and I have done a good job during internship.

Signature: Date:

中文版：

求职申请表

序号：1

申请职位：前台接待员

个人基本情况	姓名：王丽		英文名：Catherine	
	出生地：武汉		身高（厘米）：163	
	出生日期：1989年7月1日		体重（公斤）：50	
	身份证号码：420109198907011943		性别：女	
	母亲姓名：张红		婚姻状态：未婚	
	父亲姓名：王刚		国籍：中国	
教育背景	学校名称（中学/专科/本科）	起止日期		专业
		年　月	年　月	
	武汉职业技术学院	2008年9月	2010年6月	酒店管理
培训经历	深圳皇冠假日酒店	2009年7月	2009年9月	

所获奖励：

2010年获武汉职业技术学院英语演讲比赛二等奖

特长：

英语说、写很出色；

精通 Word，Excel，PowerPoint 之类的办公软件；

擅长游泳

工作经历	酒店/公司名称	起止日期		职位
		年　月	年　月	
	深圳皇冠假日酒店	2009年7月	2010年7月	前台接待员

工作描述：

　　作为一名前台接待员，我主要负责为客人办理入住登记和离店手续，为客人分配房间，以及接听客人的预订电话。此外，因工作需要，我还要做一些有关收银和审计方面的工作，比如为各类会议准备账目。在实习期间，我凭借自己的责任感和认真仔细的态度出色地完成了各项工作。

签名：　　　　　　　　　　　　　　　　　　　　　　　　　　　　　　　　　日期：

1.2 英语情景对话(Dialogue)

1.2.1 Job Hunting Materials

(Chen, a senior students, is looking for a job. And now he is talking with Cathy, one of his classmates, who has just landed a job.)

Cathy: Hi, Chen, what's wrong with you? You are looking so worried.

Chen: Nothing serious. Just the job. You know, the very famous Starwood hotels group will set an job fair[1] on our campus, and I have been informed[2] that there are some positions like receptionist and management trainee available. Working for that hotel group is kind of the dream for me. I have been trying to work out[3] a schedule for hunting there.

Cathy: Well, that's fantastic. And what time for the job fair?

Chen: Tomorrow morning. And even I am not sure whether I have prepared well or not. That is why I feel so nervous. I was told that you have already got a great job, so could you give me some advice?

Cathy: Sure. Before you get into that job fair, you need to make sure that the materials for it are fully prepared.

Chen: Materials? What are the materials you are talking about?

Cathy: I mean a lot of things which can support yourself. Firstly, resume and cover letters are absolutely[4] necessary. And then the references and certificates[5] also can help a lot.

Chen: Oh, yes. I have got all these stuff prepared in my hands. Could you please do me a favor to go through them?

Cathy: Definitely. Let me see. Oh, all these are ok. But there is a question in my mind.

Chen: What?

Cathy: You just mentioned that you really want to get a job in the Starwood hotels group. Is that an international one?

Chen: Of course, look at the brochure[6]. It reads: Starwood Hotels Group is one of the leading hotel and leisure companies in the world with more than 700 properties in more than 80 countries and 110,000 employees at its owned and managed properties. With internationally renowned[7] brands, Starwood is a fully integrated owner, operator and franchisor of hotels and resorts, including St. Regis, The Luxury Collection, Sheraton, Westin, Four Points by Sheraton, as well as Starwood Vacation Ownership, Inc., one of the premier developers and operators of high quality vacation interval ownership resorts.

Cathy: Ok, since the group is such a multi-national[8] one, I think the English version of the materials is really indispensable[9].

Chen: Oh, how silly I am, I even didn't realize the importance of the English version. I really appreciate[10] your reminding. The whole package should be done by tomorrow. Time is clocking here. I get to run.

Cathy: You can make it. Good luck.

Notes:

[1] job fair:工作招聘会　例:Graduation is three months away and students are desperate to compete for the posts on offer at job fair.（距离毕业还有三个月的时间，大学生们都非常希望能够在招聘会上找到一份工作。）

[2] inform:告知,通知　例:Computer can inform the travelers of the weather condition.（电脑可以让度假的人了解天气情况。）

[3] work out:想出,解决,弄懂　例:They seize upon whatever is at hand, work out their problem, and master the situation.（他们紧紧抓住现有的机会,解决他们的问题,掌控自己的局面。）

[4] absolutely:绝对正确,正是如此　例:Carol has a good job, but contributes nothing and has absolutely no responsibilities.（卡罗尔虽然有一份好的工作,但是对这个家却难言尽责。）

[5] certificate:单据,凭证,证明书　例:Foreign students accepted at an

American school will receive a document called a Certificate of Eligibility. （得到美国学校承认的外国学生将收到一份被称为资格证书的文件。）

[6] brochure：手册，宣传手册　例：Enclosed is our latest new products brochure. （内附我公司最新产品手册。）

[7] renowned：有名的，闻名的　例：This college is renowned for its football team. （这所大学因其足球队而闻名。）

[8] multi-national：多国的，跨国的　例：One multi-national is already implementing a program. （一个跨国公司已经在实施一个计划。）

[9] indispensable：必需元素，不可或缺的　例：Health is indispensable to everyone. （健康是人人所必要的。）

[10] appreciate：赏识，欣赏，感谢　例：I really appreciate your help. （我真的很感谢你的帮助。）

1.2.2 What information do you need?

(Chen is talking with his Career Guidance about some interview issues.)

Chen：Mr Li, sorry to interrupt you, may I speak with you for a while?

Li：Sure, Chen, what can I do for you?

Chen：I will attend a job fair on our campus tomorrow, which wears me out and I really want the job so badly. Mr Li, are there any tips[1] to get the job?

Li：Just relax, don't take too much pressure[2] on you. Speaking of the tips towards job interview, I do have some.

Chen：Perfect, I am all ears[3].

Li：Ok! First of all, if you want to join the targeted company, the more you know about the company and the job, the more chances you would get.

Chen：That sounds great. But how can I suppose to know about my targeted company? It seems very difficult for me.

Li：Well, actually, it is not that hard, you can start with conducting good background[4] research on the targeted company. And there are so many items on the Company research checklist you need to know.

Chen: What are the items?

Li: The most important is the company's products and service.

Chen: Why is that so important?

Li: Because interviewers want to know specifically[5] why you want to join their company-your motivation[6] or your drive. If you know more about the company's products and service, you could perform more intelligently[7] and confidently.

Chen: I see, besides these, are there any other things I need to pay attention to?

Li: Absolutely yes. The company culture is also important. It mainly consists of[8] company mission, vision[9], value statements.

Chen: Oh, that's to say the company culture is what a presentation the organization profiles[10] itself, right?

Li: Yes. You are so smart. Equipped with this information, you could customize your performance at interview to show your sincerity to work for this company and your suitableness as an employee-to-be.

Chen: But there is still one problem, that is, how can I get all this information?

Li: The most effective way is to get access to the company's official website, which can be very resourceful for you.

Chen: Oh, it seems I have a lot of homework to do.

Li: You bet. One can never be too well prepared.

Notes:

[1] tip: 窍门，小费，给小费　例: The main tip is to gain bargaining power by understanding the person on the other side of the table.（主要的窍门是通过了解谈判桌对面的人(对手)来增进讨价还价的能力。）

[2] pressure: 压力，施压，迫使　例: If the pressure builds up excessively, the pressure valve opens to relieve the pressure.（如果油箱内压力过高,则压力阀开启,以降低压力。）

[3] I am all ears: 固定用语表示"洗耳恭听"　例: Tell me your story, I am all ears.（告诉我你的故事,我洗耳恭听。）

[4] background：背景，后台，基础　　例：My work experience and education background have supplied me with many skills and an understanding of dealing with the teenagers．（我有很好的教育背景和丰富的工作经历，并因此懂得许多与青少年打交道的技巧。）

[5] specifically：明确的，特别的，具体的　　例：You were specifically warned not to eat fish．（已经特别叮嘱过你不要吃鱼。）

[6] motivation：动机，动力　　例：Motivation is the leading affection factor contributing to language learning．（动机是影响语言学习最重要的内部因素。）

[7] intelligently：聪明的，智慧的　　例：We are trying to show the way for the business world to give intelligently and to support us with more than just money．（我们正试图向商界展现这种方式，要聪明地给予，而不仅仅是为我们提供资金支持。）

[8] consist of：由…组成　　例：The throwing events consist of javelin, discus, hammer and shot．（投掷项目包括标枪、铁饼、链球和铅球。）

[9] vision：远景，景象，设想　　例：Indeed, his vision is rather similar to Gruen's．（的确，他与格伦的设想如出一辙.）

[10] profiles：轮廓，形象，描绘　　例：She has tried to profile a man typical of New York．（她试图扼要描写一个典型的纽约人。）

1.3　学以致用（Transference）

1. 假如你即将要去参加一场招聘会，下列表格中有哪些材料是你认为应该带去的，请说明理由。

| Advertisement　　Awards　　Brochure of your college/university　　Certificate |
| CV/Resume　　Designing　　Diploma　　Cover letter　　Driving license |
| Electronic dictionary　　Family photo　　Graduation project　　I. D. Card |
| Laptop computer/P. D. A　　Name card　　Pen　　Publications　　Recommendation letter |
| Thesis　　School report　　Reference from teachers or previous employers |
| Video of performance　　Gift　　Trophy　　Money　　Notebook　　Calculator |

2. 请为下列中文网站名称找出相对应的网址,并将其连线。

(1) 中华英才网　　　　　A. www.google.com

(2) 谷歌搜索引擎　　　　B. www.51job.com

(3) 前程无忧网　　　　　C. www.zhaopin.com

(4) 智联招聘网　　　　　D. www.baidu.com

(5) 百度搜索引擎　　　　E. www.chinahr.com

3. 阅读下列句子,并将其按正确的顺序排列成一段短文。

A. The single best resource is probably to go online to the company's website.

B. Type the company's name in the search box and follow the link to the company's website.

C. Scroll through all the information, and make notes of details you want to remember.

D. The company's information can be sourced in a number of ways.

E. Go to your favorite search engine, such as www.google.com.

4. Listen to the following passages, and then fill in the blanks.

What Can You Get from Company Websites?

Company websites usually feature ___(1)___ information on the organization. Read it all, even media ___(2)___ and staff biographies. Look specifically for information on ___(3)___ culture, upcoming opportunities and ___(4)___ and latest results.

Search on the company website for any details relevant to the ___(5)___ you are being interviewed for. Look at the ___(6)___ department and staff who work there.

Search on the company website for information about the ___(7)___. If you are being sent to a company interview by a recruiter, ask them to give you ___(8)___ about the interviewer and any other job interview information you need.

If the company does not have its own site there are ___(9)___ sites that have extensive information about companies and industries. Simply type in the company name and use the different search ___(10)___s to go to sites that have details on the company.

5. 快速阅读下列短文,并完成练习。

Three key Questions for Self-orientation

Nowadays, in order to launch the career right in a pretty intense job market, it is critical for college students to set an accurate self-orientation for themselves based on the career planning theory accordingly. After the precise self-orientation, they can not only strengthen their own understanding towards themselves better, but also can they find out the potential working fields which their interests really lie in ①. To set one's self-orientation accurately, here come the 3 key questions you might really think about it.

Firstly, _____. To answer the question right, you probably need to figure out what professional knowledge have you learned during your education path and what kinds of social practice you have ever involved in as well. By doing this, it really can help you to decide your own career direction at some extent. It is undeniable that getting the professional knowledge as much as you could is one of the premise conditions of career planning ②.

Secondly, _____. We are talking about life experience here. Experience is the one's most valuable wealth, it can not only reflect one's qualities and potential status, but also plays a crucial role in job hunting process ③. Sometimes, for a job-candidate, experience is more important than professional knowledge itself, because many things only experienced, you can make your own point about it.

Finally, _____. Conducting a thorough analysis of the cases you consider highly achieved ④. By doing so, you can find the superior side of yourself—some extraordinary personalities which others may don't have, such as persistent, decisive or even a big great heart. But that's not enough; you need to mine your power source and charm sparkle continuously based on these extraordinary personalities or qualities you have to form the supporting rock for your career planning. Using your own advantages as a weapon to step the career path, it can never be wrong ⑤.

(1) 请正确将下面三句话放到文中空白处,使课文完整通顺。

  A. What is the most successful thing you have been achieved?

  B. What have you been experienced?

C. What have you learned?

(2) 将文中画线部分翻译成中文。

① _____.

② _____.

③ _____.

④ _____.

⑤ _____.

1.4 补充英语阅读(Reading)

1. 阅读下列课文并为其找出最合适的标题。

   A. Traditional Ways to Get Job Information

   B. Five Different Ways to Get Job Information

   C. The best Way to Get Job Information

   D. The Modern Job Market

2. 根据课文内容判断正(T)误(F)。

   (1) In these modern times, people would like to change their jobs frequently. (   )

   (2) In the old days, people used to look solely at the newspaper want-ads to find their dream jobs. (   )

   (3) If you already have your dream employer in mind, you should call the employer directly to find the information you need. (   )

   (4) You can combine several different ways to find great job opportunities. (   )

   (5) Temporary employment can never lead to permanent positions. (   )

The old days of finding a job right out of school and sticking with it until retirement are certainly in the past. In these modern times, people have become more adept at locating new job opportunities. But some of the more traditional tactics[1] have started to fade in popularity; no longer are people looking solely at the newspaper want ads[2] to find their dream jobs. Job seekers are becoming more creative and utilizing[3] new strategies in moving their careers forward. Here are some ways:

Firstly, job fairs. They are typically targeted toward specific industries, though some job or recruitment fairs are more generalized. These ads will usually come with a list of the organizations that will be present. Investigate[4] any companies that interest you, bring a number of resumes and be ready to sell yourself.

Secondly, career websites. You can use job search engines on the Internet or the vast number of career-related websites that post job openings, such as www.51job.com or www.zhaopin.com. These websites function[5] in a similar way to the traditional want ads. However, they have a much quicker turnaround time and allow you to search a much larger number of jobs over a large area.

Thirdly, company websites. If you already have your dream employer in mind, why not go directly to the career section of their website? If you watch for openings on their site, there's a chance you'll find just the opportunity that you've been waiting for. Create a list of employers that you'd like to work for and visit their websites often.

Fourthly, head hunters and recruitment agencies. If you're looking for some professional help in your job search, head hunters and recruitment agencies can definitely lend a hand. There are a number of organizations that hire through recruitment agencies because it helps to streamline[6] the lengthy process of locating and interviewing candidates. Head hunters locate individuals to fill a specific vacancy[7] within an organization or find a position for a job seeker who has hired their services.

Finally, temping[8] or internships. Sometimes temporary employment can lead to permanent[9] positions. If you're without work, finding a temporary position with a great company is a great way to get a foot in the door, or provide you with useful business contacts to call upon in the future. Internships are a great choice for students who are just graduating from college and many schools' job placement services can connect students with opportunities.

In the modern job market, finding the very best job opportunities often requires a combination of methods. Always keep in mind that there are a variety of methods available[10] for finding job opportunities, all with their own strengths and weaknesses, so don't be shy to experiment with a variety of techniques.

Notes:

［1］tactic:战术;策略;手法　例:The new tactic was put into operation in 1939.（这个新的战略是在1939年初开始运用的。）

［2］want ads:招聘广告　例:She is scanning the want ads and looking for a job.（她正在浏览招聘广告找工作。）

［3］utilize:利用　例:Scientists are trying to find more efficient ways of utilizing solar energy.（科学家正在寻找能更有效地利用太阳能的方法。）

［4］investigate:调查,研究,侦查　例:They investigate corruption, observe elections and watch for government influence over the media.（他们调查腐败,监督选举以及关注政府对媒体的影响。）

［5］function:功能,用途,职能　例:We may provide flexible customize and various operation random extend function for customer.（可为用户提供灵活的定制与多业务任意扩展的功能。）

［6］streamline:流线型,使……流线型化　例:The draft tries to streamline the registration of property sales and make it easier for interested parties to check details.（此法案试图使得产权的登记更加流线合理化,有利于购买方核查。）

［7］vacancy:空房,空缺,空位　例:I see a vacancy board outside for a kitchen helper. Is it still available?（我在外面招工牌上看到有个厨房帮手的空缺。这空位现在还有吗?）

［8］temp:临时雇员,做临时工作　例:Temping is a great way to build contacts.（打临时工,是建立人际关系的良方。）

［9］permanent:永久的,永恒的,不变的　例:He has no permanent employment.（他没有永久性的工作。）

［10］available:可获得的,可利用的,可得到的　例:Unfortunately, the team did not have a suitable group of Africans available for study.（不幸的是,这个团队并没有一组合适的非洲人作为研究对象。）

第二章 英文求职简历 (Resume or Curriculum Vitae)

案例导入(Lead-in)

小张和小刘同为某高校酒店管理专业的应届毕业生,她们同时向某五星级国际知名酒店集团投掷了简历。虽然她们目标相同,但对于简历的制作却各持己见。小张认为简历应面面俱到,从各方面反映自身的优势。于是她将自己从中学至大学的所有获奖情况一一罗列,并附上相应的荣誉证书,使得简历厚达8页之多,且并未制作英文简历。小刘认为简历应该目标明确,重点突出,于是她仅用一页的篇幅描述了所有与申请职位相关的个人资料,并提供了简历的英文版本。在小刘投完简历3天后,便接到了面试通知,而小张却一直未收到面试通知。

问题1:你认为小张没有收到面试通知的原因是什么?

问题2:你认为小刘能够接到面试通知的原因有哪些?

2.1 学习焦点(Focus)

英文简历是用英语来介绍自己的个人资料、学历、工作经历、能力、业绩、性格、业余爱好等情况的书面报告,是求职择业时最为重要的材料。绝大部分外资企业会根据英文简历提供的情况决定是否给予求职者面试机会,且面试后也会将其作为是否聘用的重要依据。英文简历可以用好几个词语来表达,例如 Resume、Curriculum Vitae、Personal History 等。在英国,人们习惯用 Curriculum Vitae(通常缩写为 CV)来表示简历。在美国,人们以前一般用 Personal History,偶尔也用 Data

Sheet,不过现在则通用 Resume 这个单词。Resume 一词来源于法语,因此当你应聘法资企业时也可使用该单词。

2.1.1 英文简历的构成要素(Essential Elements)

尽管英文简历的内容和风格往往会因人因岗而异,但总的来讲,其有五大基本构成要素,即:页眉部分、求职意向、教育背景、工作经历和个人资料。下面,就分别从这五个部分来对英文简历进行介绍。

2.1.1.1 英文简历页眉部分(Heading)

英文简历的页眉部分主要包括求职人姓名、地址和电话。此外,也可以将求职目标放在姓名和地址的下面,以说明自己想求取的职位。但如果求职人并不清楚用人单位有哪些职位空缺,或觉得自己能够胜任用人单位的多种工作时,也可以不写这部分。

(1)求职人姓名(Name)。在英文简历中,求职人姓名有很多种写法。如果求职者在国内求职,就可以按照中国人的姓名顺序将姓写在前,名写在后。例如:求职人的姓名为刘晓虎,可采用"Liu Xiaohu"的写法。这是因为国际标准化组织已认可我国的人名和地名按照汉语拼音的顺序拼写。当然,如果在英语国家求职,由于部分外国人的确不知道中国人姓名的特点,求职人就应该按照国际惯例,大写姓的每一个字母,或给姓加下划线,如:LIU Xiaohu 或 Liu Xiaohu。

(2)英文简历地址(Address)。英文地址的书写顺序与中文地址刚好相反,是由小到大排列,即:门牌号—街道—城市—省(自治区、直辖市)—邮政编码—国家。简历中的地址既可以写成一行,又可分行写。例如:"湖北省武汉市关山大道463号,邮政编码430074"有如下两种写法。

第一种:463 Guanshan Road, Wuhan, Hubei 430074 PRC

第二种:463 Guanshan Road

　　　　Wuhan, Hubei 430074

　　　　P. R. C.

需要注意的是,门牌号的前面不加 No. 或 #;Road,street,Boulevard,Lane 等词,不要缩写;邮政编码应放在省(自治区、直辖市)的后面,之间不用逗号;国家名称可写成 China,PRC,P. R. C. 或 The People's Republic of China。

(3)电话(Telephone)。电话的写法很讲究,有以下四点值得大家注意。

A. 如果是向驻境外企业求职,电话号码前一定要加地区号,例如:求职人所在地为武汉,即在电话号码前加86-27。

B. 如果电话号码为8位数,当中最好加一个"-",如6505-2266,便于拨号。

C. 应在区号后的括号和号码间加空格,如(86-10) 8765-4321。这是英文写作格式的规定。

D. 写手机号码时同向别人通报手机号码一样,应遵循"3-4-4原则",如"135-4567-1234"。

2.1.1.2 求职目标(Job Objective)

求职目标是锁定一个具体职位最简单、最迅速的方法。当然,也有人认为在简历里加上求职目标不仅占空间,还会把你限制在某个职位上,当你其实适合于多个职位的时候。但无论怎样,了解求职目标的写作方法是一种明智之举。

如有求职目标,应将其放在姓名和联系方式的下面,以 Objective, Job Objective, Career Objective 或 Professional Objective 引导。求职目标一定要简短、最多不超过两到三行。通常典型的求职目标以名词短语或不定式短语表示。例如:

A. Job Objective:Waitress(应聘职位:餐厅服务员)

B. Career Objective:Position as a supervisor at the Front Desk(应聘职位:前厅部主管)

C. Objective:To obtain a responsible position in financial management in the hospitality industry(求职目标:酒店业财务管理的负责职位)

求职者在发简历申请职位之前应检查求职目标,确保它适合所申请的职位。如果有多个求职目标,那就应该相应地准备多个不同版本的求职简历。

2.1.1.3 教育背景(Education Backgroud)

教育背景以 Education Backgroud 为标题,列出自上大学以来或上职业技术学校以来受教育的情况,是每份简历必然涉及的内容。对于有工作经验的求职者,可以把教育背景置于工作经历部分的后面,简单说明基本情况即可。而对于毕业生,由于缺乏工作经验,则可以用强调所掌握的知识和技能以及所修过的相关课程来丰富这一部分。下面,有关教育背景的写法有几点值得注意。

(1)时间(Period)。时间要倒序,将最近的学历情况要放在最前面。

(2)学校名称(Graduate College/University)。学校名称需要大写并加粗,以便招聘者迅速识别求职者的学历。

(3)社会工作(Social Activities)。如在校期间担任过班干部,只写职务就可以了;如参加过社团协会,则写明职务和社团名,如果什么职务都没有,就写"member of club(s)"。社团协会,在国外一般都用 club。关于这一部分,不必写明年月和工作详情,有些可留待工作经历中写。

(4)奖学金(Scholarship)。对于有工作经验的人,一般仅用一句话概括自己所获的奖学金情况。如果有多个,也尽量用一句话概括。但如果是毕业生,则可以对获奖情况详细描述。

(5)成绩(Achievement)。除非是前十名,否则建议不写成绩,以便让人觉得你的成绩不够优秀。

Education Backgroud:

2009 – 2011: Master in Tourism Management, MBA

              Hubei University, Wuhan

              Major Courses:

              High-level Economic Study, Financial Management of Tourism Business, Advanced Management, Strategic Management, Research Methods and Theory of Tourism Industry, Research on Tourism Information System, Spanish

2005 – 2009: Bachelor of Arts in English

              Hubei University, Wuhan

Awards: Top Scholarship, 2007, 2008

        Excellent Student Leader, 2008, 2009

Activities: President, Student Council of English Departmet

教育背景:

2009 – 2011:湖北大学工商管理硕士(旅游管理方向)

              主修课程:高级西方经济学、旅游企业财务管理、高级管理学、企业战略管理、旅游产业理论与研究方法、旅游信息系统研究、西班牙语

2005 – 2009：湖北大学英语专业文学学士

获奖情况：2007 年和 2008 年获一等奖学金

2008 年和 2009 年被评为"优秀学生干部"

担任职务：英语系学生会主席

2.1.1.4 工作经历(Working Experience)

工作经历主要反映求职人工作过的单位名称及其所在的省市名称、就职和离职时间、担任的行政职务或技术职务、主要工作职责及业绩。这部分常见的标题包括 Experience, Work Experience, Professional Experience, Career Highlights, Employment History 或 Employment Record 等。特别强调的是，对于正在工作的人，应将工作经历写在教育背景的前面，以示突出自己的业绩与成就；而对于在校生，则应将教育背景放在工作经历之前。

一般情况下，多采用倒叙的方法列出工作经历。即：先写现在的工作，再依次写过去的工作。如：

Working Experience：

2004 – 2006：The Great Wall Sheraton Hotel Beijing

  PR & Marketing Manager

  Duties and responsibilities included：

  a. Developing and delivering marketing strategy for the property

  b. plan and manage its implementation, liaising closely with key stakeholders (General Manager, Sales Team, Department heads)

2002 – 2004：Park Hyatt Dubai, United Arab Emirates

  Sale and Marketing Assistant

  Duties and responsibilities included：

  a. Assisting the Sales and Marketing Manager in mapping out potential customers and competitors

  b. Research new market opportunities

  c. Continually help promote up-selling and cross-selling of all hotel services

工作经历：

2004—2006：北京喜来登长城酒店

    公关销售经理

    负责业务：

    a. 为酒店研究和提交营销策略方案

    b. 制订实施方案，监管实施活动，并及时向酒店的主要利益相关者（总经理、销售小组、各部门负责人）进行汇报。

2002—2004：阿联酋迪拜 Park Hyatt 酒店

    销售助理

    负责业务：

    a. 协助销售部经理挖掘潜在客户及竞争对手

    b. 研究新的市场机会

    c. 针对酒店所有的服务产品及项目不断优化"升级销售"和"交叉销售"的方法及手段

  如果求职者目前所从事的工作与应聘职位不相关，但以前所从事过的工作却能说明求职者有胜任应聘职位的能力，则应先写出那段最具说服力的经历。

  对于求职择业的毕业生而言，在这一部分中应写出其课外兼职和实习经历，以提供求职成功的可能性。例如：

Summer, 2006 Receptionist

       Ramada Plaza Optics Valley Hotel Wuhan

       Duties: provided information for the guests, helped them solve problem

Summer, 2004 Waitress

       Pizza Hut, Zhongnan Road, Wuhan

       Duties: received guests, recommended food, collected feed-back

2006 年暑假 在武汉光谷华美达大酒店实习

      任前台接待员

      主要职责：为客人提供信息并帮助客人解决问题

2004 年暑假	在武汉中南路必胜客餐厅兼职
	任餐厅服务员
	主要职责:迎接客人,为客人推荐餐饮,收集客人反馈意见

2.1.1.5 个人资料(Personal Information)

个人资料是除了上述三大部分之外其他与求职相关的个人信息,包括性别(Sex/Gender)、出生日期(Date of Birth)、出生地点(Birthplace)、国籍或民族(Nationality)、身高(Height)、体重(Weight)、婚姻状况(Marital Status)、子女人数(Number of Children)、健康状况(Health Condition)、技能(Skills)、业余爱好(Hobbies)以及会员资格(Membership)等。通常一份简历的容量有限,求职者在此部分中应该突出重点,少列为宜。但特别强调的是,由于酒店业是一个注重求职者外在职业形象的行业,尤其是某些部门对员工的身高和体重有一定要求,因此在个人资料中最好注明身高和体重。例如:

Birth Date: January 20, 1988　　　　Sex: Female
Height: 166cm　　　　　　　　　　Weight: 55kg
Health: Excellent　　　　　　　　　Marital Status: Single
Hobbies: Chinese literature, singing, basketball
Skills: Excellent in English speaking and writing
　　　　Expert at Office Programs such as Word, Excel, PowerPoint
Membership: Member, Hubei Tourism Association
出生日期:1988 年 1 月 20 日　　　　性别:女
身高:166 厘米　　　　　　　　　　体重:55 公斤
身体状况:健康　　　　　　　　　　婚姻状况:未婚
兴趣爱好:中国文学、唱歌、打篮球
专项技能:英语说、写很出色
　　　　精通 Word,Excel,PowerPoint 之类的办公软件
会员资格:湖北旅游协会会员

如果求职者的专项技能比较丰富,可将其从个人资料中抽离并单独纳入一项,作为简历中的独立部分,以重点突出自己的优势和特长。

英文简历除了上述的五大部分之外,有时还需要2~3名证明人,以强调其内容的真实性。证明人应具有一定的社会信誉和威望。求职者事先应征得他们的同意。这部分以 Reference 为标题,列出证明人的姓名、职务、地址和联系电话即可。

2.1.2 学生简历的撰写技巧(How to Write a Student Resume)

我们之所以要把学生简历单独拿出来讨论,是因为学生的工作经验较少,简历页面内容不够丰满,故不宜按照之前所介绍的格式来撰写简历。在此,特别介绍一些学生简历撰写技巧。

(1)篇幅适中(Sized Properly)。一个企业,尤其是大企业在招聘期内会收到很多份简历,工作人员不可能对每份简历都仔细研读,一般而言,阅读一份简历只占用一分钟时间,再长的简历也不超过三分钟。所以,建议学生简历的篇幅尽量控制在一页纸内。

(2)目标明确(High-lighted)。不少人力资源专家都认为,学生的求职简历上一定要注明应聘的职位。学生由于缺乏丰富的工作经验,如果把自己定位为"万金油"(Jake of all Trades),既不现实,又容易让人反感。所以,在简历中应突出自己在某一方面的优点,不能把自己说成是一个全才,任何职位都适合。建议每份简历都要根据申请的职位来设计,并根据工作性质有侧重地表现自己。如果你认为同一家企业有两个职位都适合你,可以向该企业同时投两份简历。

(3)有的放矢(Focused)。简历的内容一定要具有针对性。求职者可以针对某特定的职位要求修改自己的简历,尽量让自己提供的信息与企业的需要相符。这就需要求职者在撰写简历前对所应聘的企业认真做一番调查,仔细阅读招聘广告,然后加强简历内容与职位要求的相关性。

(4)重点突出(Well Presented)。英文简历中,专业经历(实习和暑期兼职)部分是重头戏。因为这个部分是面试官最感兴趣和关心的,以后即使在面试时,也差不多围绕这个在讨论。写简历时,应尽可能花大"手笔"去描述这个部分。即便没有兼职经历,就算只是在父母单位待过几天,也不妨写上。这样也算是接触过社会,了解了一些行业,做过了一些工作。但前提是,一定要能说上几句才写在简历上。否则将来面试时,会被考官问得张口结舌,适得其反。另外,在教育背景部分中,学生可以注明相关的课程。但千万不要为了拼凑篇幅,把所有的课程都写上,也不要将中学经历都写了上去,这样既显累赘拖沓,别人也没耐心看。

(5)用事实说话(Supported by Facts)。描述个人成就时,应列举相关实例,以增加说服力。介绍个人技能时,要突出如何将技能发挥到工作中去。且每个技能后要加上简要介绍,以方便招聘者直接浏览。面试时,也可以更深入地谈谈这些技能。

(6)包装得当(Well laid-out)。除非应聘美术设计、装潢、广告等专业,一般来说学生简历不必做得太花哨。用质量较好的 A4 白纸即可。此外,若简历上出现错别字或是在格式、排版上有技术性错误以及简历被折叠得皱皱巴巴、有污点,会给用人单位留下做事不认真的印象,这是求职的一大忌讳。因此,在投递简历前一定要认真检查每一个细节,做到一丝不苟。

(7)注重文化差异性(Focusing on cultural differences)。不同国家因文化差异性对简历也有着不同要求,因而在制作简历前应该事先了解国家间的文化差异,从而达到事半功倍的效果。例如,美国企业不要求求职者主动提供年龄、婚姻状况和家庭情况,这些都属于个人隐私;在英国,求职者可以不提供出生年月以及婚姻状况。

2.1.3 英文简历的常用语句(Useful Expressions for Resume)

2.1.3.1 求职目标(Job Objective)

(1)To obtain an entry-level position as a hotel receptionist with active involvement in the areas of event planning and office management.

获得像酒店接待员这样的初级职位,并积极参与活动策划和办公室管理方面的事务。

(2) A position as guest service agent utilizing my training in business administration, building relationships with hotel guests and providing superior customer service.

客服代表的职位,能运用我在企业管理方面的培训知识,与酒店客户建立良好关系,并能为客人提供优质的服务。

(3)a position as a Bartender in a well know hotel where it can benefit from my 12 years extensive experience, creativeness, multi-tasking abilities, strong interpersonal skills, a positive attitude and a good knowledge of the bar scene.

一家知名酒店的酒吧调酒师,能用上12年的丰富经验、创造力、多头任务处理能力、较强的交际能力、积极的态度以及精湛的酒吧工作知识。

(4) A position as an administrative assistant to an executive where communication skills and enthusiasm towards others will be assets.

高级管理人员的行政助理,用得上交际技巧和热情待人的态度。

(5) a position as a manager in a reputed hotel where I can use my experience as well as the knowledge which I have gained during my experience and my dynamic personality to manage the hotel in best possible way.

一家知名酒店的经理,能凭借积累的经验、已获取的知识以及充沛的精力以最好的方式来管理好酒店。

(6) To secure a challenging position with an ABC Hotel that will utilize my problem solving, planning and budget management abilities.

在ABC酒店中谋求一个有挑战性的职位,以发挥我解决问题、计划和预算管理的能力。

2.1.3.2 受教育程度(Education)

(1) Majored in hotel management. Courses included: hotel English, theory of hotel management, managing Food and Beverage operations, managing Front Office operations, managing Housekeeping operations, marketing in hospitality industry, accounting, cross-culture communication in Tourism, customer relationship management.

主修酒店管理专业。课程包括:酒店英语、酒店管理概论、餐饮部运行与管理、前厅部运行与管理、客房部运行与管理、旅游市场营销、会计学、旅游跨文化交际、客户关系管理。

(2) Curriculum completed: food and beverage management, 90; supervision in the hospitality industry, 86; basic financial accounting for the hospitality industry, 89; facilities management, 87; managing for quality in the hospitality industry, 88; resort management and development, 90; international hotel management, 92; bar and

beverage Management, 89; food and beverage cost controls, 89; hospitality industry computer systems, 91; hospitality sales and marketing, 90.

所修课程:餐饮管理,90 分;酒店业督导实务,86 分;酒店业会计学基础,89 分;酒店设备管理,87 分;酒店质量管理,88 分;度假地管理与开发,90 分;国际酒店管理概论,92 分;酒水与饮料管理,89 分;餐饮成本控制,89 分;酒店计算机操作系统,91 分;酒店市场营销,90 分。

(3) Minored in economics. Courses covered are as follows: public finance, macroeconomics, microeconomics, industrial organization and international economics.

辅修经济学涉及的课程有:公共财物金融学、宏观经济学、微观经济学、工业组织学和国际经济学。

(4) Major courses contributing to management qualification: management, accounting, economics, marketing, sociology.

对管理资格有帮助的主要课程:管理学、会计学、经济学、市场学、社会学。

(5) Among the pertinent courses I have taken are: office administration, secretarial procedures, business communication, psychology, data-processing, typing, shorthand.

在相关的课程中我修过的有:办公室管理、秘书程序、商务交际、心理学、资料处理、打字、速记。

(6) Courses taken that would be useful for computer programming are: computer science, systems design and analysis, FORTRAN programming, PASCAL programming, operating systems, systems management.

对计算机编程有用的课程有:计算机学、系统设计与分析、FORTRAN 编程学、PASCAL 编程学、操作系统、系统管理。

(7) Master in Tourism Management, MBA, 1999 to 2002, Wuhan University.

工商管理硕士(旅游管理方向),1999 年至 2002 年,于武汉大学学习。

(8) The Bachelor of International Hotel Management, 2003 to 2005, Ecole hocteliere de Lausanne.

国际酒店管理学士,2003 年至 2005 年,于瑞士洛桑酒店管理学院学习。

2.1.3.3 工作经历(Working Experience)

(1) Sales manager. In addition to ordinary sales activities and management of

department, responsible for recruiting and training of sales staff members.

销售部经理。除了正常销售活动和部门管理之外,还负责招聘与训练销售人员。

(2)2007 – 2010,Manager,Chinese Restaurant, Ramada Plaza Optics Valley Hotel Wuhan. Supervised operation of 180 – seat restaurant. Directed opening of Hubei – style catering business, which added 20% annually to restaurant profits.

2007年至2010年,在武汉光谷华美达大酒店中餐厅任经理。管理拥有180个席位的餐厅运营。负责开展具有湖北风格的酒席承担业务,从而使该餐厅的年利润增加20%。

(3) Tourist guide during the summer vacation for Xi'an International Travel Agency. Conducted tours for foreign tourists on trip around the city.

暑假期间在西安国际旅行社当导游。负责外国游客在城区的观光旅游。

(4)Worked 18 hours weekly as a Sales Manager at the student – run coffee shop of Wuhan Technic College in 2011 and increased the sales volime by 40%. Earn 30% of college expense.

于2011年在武汉职业技术学院学生自主经营的咖啡厅里担任销售经理,每周工作18小时,并使销售额上升40%,挣了大学学费的30%。

(5) Secretary to president of Tian'an Holiday Inn Wuhan. Responsibilities: Receiving visitors, arranging meeting, taking and typing dictation, writing routine letters and reports.

在武汉天安假日酒店任董事长秘书。职责:接待访客、安排会议、笔录并打字、书写日常信函及报告。

(6)From 2004 till now working at Hubei University, teaching Hotel Management.

自2004年至今在湖北大学工作,主讲酒店管理。

2.1.3.4 任职资格(Qualifications)

(1) Diploma in Hotel Management (2003); Band – 6 College English Test (2002); English Guide ID Card(2003).

2003年获酒店管理大专文凭;2002年通过全国大学英语6级统考;2003年获英语导游证。

(2) I am experience in operating OPERA and modern office equipments.

本人能熟练操作酒店管理信息系统(OPERA)以及现代办公设备。

(3) I have got a bilingual Tourist Guide ID Card and a driving license.

我获得了双语导游证和驾照。

(4) I have a chef license. Especially, I am expert at Guangdong cuisine.

我有厨师证书。我尤其擅长粤菜烹饪技术。

(5) Ability to organize marketing campaigns and to supervise employees. Effective communication abilities and public relations skills.

具有组织市场活动和督导员工的能力,并具有效的交际能力和公关技巧。

(6) Special training in management at Shangri-La Training Center and three years of practical experience as an assistant lobby manager. Enjoy working with people. Responsible and reliable.

在香格里拉酒店培训中心接受管理方面的专门培训,并有三年大堂副理的实际工作经验。喜欢和别人一同工作。负责可靠。

(7) Good at typing, shorthand and administrative work. Able to handle all international communications in English.

擅长打字、速记和行政工作。能用英语处理所有的国际通信。

(8) I graduated from hospitality school, and I know how to treat our guests quickly and properly.

我毕业于餐旅管理学校,所以我懂得如何迅速且正确地招呼客人。

(9) Having good memories and organizational skills to keep track of food and drink orders and the preferences of frequent restaurant patrons.

具备良好记忆力和组织能力,能记录客人的餐饮点单以及常客们对饮食的偏好。

2.1.4 英文简历实例

Example 1

RESUME

Wang Lin

Room 520, No. 458, Xu Dong Avenue, Wuhan 430000

(027) 8648 9564   wanglin@ yahoo. com. cn

EDUCATION:	Bachelor degree, Hubei University, 2006 – 2010
	Wuhan 15th High School, 2003 – 2006
Major:	Hotel management
Main Courses:	Food and Beverage Management, Supervision in the Hospitality Industry, Basic Financial Accounting for the Hospitality Industry, Managing for Quality in the Hospitality Industry
Honors and Awards:	Second-prize in college English Speech Contest (June, 2009)
	First-class college scholarship (2007 – 2009)
Certifications:	CET6 (Excellent)
	International Guide ID Card
Skills:	Excellent in English speaking and writing
	Expert at Office Programs such as Word, Excel, PowerPoint

WORKING EXPERIENCE:

    Summer, 2009　Receptionist

        Ramada Plaza Optics Valley Hotel Wuhan

        Duties: provided information for the guests, helped them solve problems

    Summer, 2008　Waitress

        Pizza Hut, Zhongnan Road, Wuhan

        Duties: received guests, recommended food, collected feed-back

Character profile: outgoing, hardworking and team-oriented

Personal data: Age 22　　Sex Female　　Health Excellent

个人简历

王　林

武汉市徐东大街 458 号 520 房间　　邮编　430000

（027）8648 9564　　　电子邮件　wanglin@ yahoo. com. cn

教育：	学士学位,湖北大学,2006—2010
	武汉市第十五中学,2003—2006
专业：	旅游管理
主要课程：	餐饮管理、酒店业督导实务、酒店业会计学基础、酒店质量管理
获奖情况：	校英语口语竞赛二等奖(2009 年 6 月)
	校一等奖学金（2007—2009）
证书：	大学英语六级证书(优秀)
	国际导游证
技能：	英语说、写很出色
	精通 Word,Excel,PowerPoint 之类的办公软件
工作经历：	
2009 年暑假	在武汉光谷华美达大酒店实习
	任前台接待员
	主要职责:为客人提供信息并帮助客人解决问题
2008 年暑假	在武汉中南路必胜客餐厅兼职
	任餐厅服务员
	主要职责:迎接客人,为客人推荐餐饮,收集客人反馈意见
性格：	性格外向,工作努力并具团队精神
个人资料：	年龄　22　性别　女　健康状况　优秀

Example 2

RESUME

Zhao Feng

463 Guanshan Avenue, Wuhan, 430064

(027)87665888   zhaofeng@yahoo.com.cn

OBJECTIVE: A Sales Manager Position with a five-star hotel, where sales experience, strong administrative, communication, and planning abilities will be used for improving the work performance.

EXPERIENCE:

2004 - 2006: The Great Wall Sheraton Hotel Beijing

PR & Marketing Manager

Duties and responsibilities included:

a. Developing and delivering marketing strategy for the property

b. plan and manage its implementation, liaising closely with key stakeholders (General Manager, Sales Team, Department heads)

2002 - 2004: Park Hyatt Dubai, United Arab Emirates

Sale and Marketing Assistant

Duties and responsibilities included:

a. Assisting the Sales and Marketing Manager in mapping out potential customers and competitors

b. Research new market opportunities

c. Continually help promote up-selling and cross-selling of all hotel services

EDUCATION: Postgraduate Program in Tourism Management, MBA, 1999 to 2002, Wuhan University. With the degree of Master

PERSONAL: Enjoy challenges and working with people.

Interested in hospitality industry.

Willing to relocate and travel.

REFERENCE: Available upon request.

第二章 英文求职简历(Resume or Curriculum Vitae)

个人简历

赵 峰

武汉市关山大道463号 邮编430064

(027)87665888 电子邮件 zhaofeng@yahoo.com.cn

求职目标:五星级酒店销售部经理职位,能运用我丰富的销售经验,有效管理、沟通和计划能力来提高工作绩效。

工作经历:

2004-2006:北京喜来登长城酒店

公关销售经理

负责业务:a. 为酒店研究和提交营销策略方案

b. 制订实施方案,监管实施活动,并及时向酒店的主要利益相关者（总经理、销售小组、各部门负责人）进行汇报

2002-2004:阿联酋迪拜 Park Hyatt 酒店

销售助理

负责业务:a. 协助销售部经理挖掘潜在客户及竞争对手

b. 研究新的市场机会

c. 针对酒店所有的服务产品及项目不断优化"升级销售"和"交叉销售"的方法及手段

教育:武汉大学工商管理硕士学位(旅游管理方向)(1999—2002).

兴趣爱好:喜欢挑战,喜欢与人交往

喜欢在酒店业工作

愿意在外地工作,喜欢旅行

证明人:如需证明人可马上提供

2.2 英语情景对话(Dialogue)

2.2.1 Some advice about resume writing

(Hong is coming to Frank, who is her English teacher for some advice about resume writing.)

Hong: Good morning, Frank. I was told that Jumeirah Hotels & Resorts, the most luxurious[1] and innovative[2] hotel group in the world, is coming to our college for recruiting. But I have no idea about the resume writing. So would you please give me some advice about it?

Frank: Sure. Before getting started, you have to ask yourself a question: what will a resume do for me?

Hong: Oh, I have never thought about it. It really puzzled me.

Frank: A good resume can be very helpful. It can enable you to assess your strengths, skills, abilities and experience thereby preparing you for the interview process.

Hong: Oh, I see. The assessment[3] you've just mentioned is what the employer wants to know about me.

Frank: Smart! So for both the employer and you, it functions[4] as a reminder after you're done interviewing.

Hong: Since the resume is so important, are there any absolute rules of resume writing?

Frank: Yes, but only a few! Almost every rule you have ever heard can be broken, if you have a very good reason. Some rules, however, are absolutes.

Hong: Really? What are they?

Frank: Four Nos: no typing errors, no errors in spelling, no lying or grandiose[5] embellishment[6], no negative information included.

Hong: I will keep these in mind. One more thing, Frank. you know different hotels or even different positions have different requirements. So, do I need more than one version of the resume?

Frank: Good question. And the answer is absolutely yes. Employers today want to know what you can do for them, so it is imperative[7] that you create a targeted resume each time you apply for an opportunity.

Hong: I see. For this interview from Jumeirah, I need to customize[8] my resume for it.

Notes:

[1] luxurious:豪华的;非常舒适的;精选的　例:They live in a very luxurious apartment building.（他们住的公寓非常豪华。）

[2] innovative:创新的　例:His approach is both innovative and thought-provoking.（他的方法是创新的和令人深思的。）

[3] assessment:评价;估计　例:Assisting with new customer credit assessment.（协助进行新客户的信用评估。）

[4] function:官能,功能,作用　例:The major function of congress is legislation.（国会的主要职能是立法。）

[5] grandiose:宏伟的,大气的　例:The church styles range from plain to grandiose.（教堂的风格从简朴到宏伟应有尽有。）

[6] embellishment:装饰;装饰品　例:You can add any embellishment you want.（您可以添加任何点缀你想要的。）

[7] imperative:必要的;紧急的;极重要的　例:We recognize the imperative need for this development.（我们认识到对这一发展的迫切需要。）

[8] customize:定做　例:We can customize products according to your needs.（我们能根据您的需要具体定做。）

2.2.2 Do I need a job objective?

(Chen is consulting with Li, his Career Consultant, about some resume issues.)

Chen: Good Afternoon, Mr. Li. Thank you for your suggestions last time. And now may I ask you something about the resume.

Li: Of course.

Chen: This morning, my classmates discussed some issues about resume. Some of them thought it was very necessary for a resume to have a job objective[1]. But some didn't so. They thought the job objective only confines[2] the applicant to a certain position, which would cause more competition and less opportunity. And right now, I'm really confused[3]. Do I need a job objective or not?

Li: Well, It depends. If you are sending your resume for a specific position at a specific company, the answer is yes. Because it can tell the reader why you are sending the resume, for example, what position or type of position you are seeking.

Chen: Oh, I see. So how can the job objective help you in the resume?

Li: It is like the thesis[4] statement of your resume. Everything you include after it should support it.

Chen: But how to write a job objective appropriately?

Li: Well, it should be very brief, does not need to be a complete sentence.

Chen: Not a complete sentence? Then what elements[5] should be involved in it?

Li: Ideally target your job objective to include job title desired, position level, field, industry, and company name.

Chen: Take myself for example. You know, Jumeirah is my dream. And I really want to work as Guest Service Agent for it. So my job objective can be said like this: a position as Guest Service Agent in Jumeirah Hotels & Resorts.

Li: That's OK. What's more, if you want your objective to be more impressive, don't forget to use the objective to tell what you can do for the company, not what you want the company to do for you... no statements like: to gain valuable experience, etc.

Chen: Oh, so in that case, I can put my objective in this way: a position as Guest Service Agent in Jumeirah Hotels & Resorts where communication skills and enthusiasm towards others will be assets.

Li: That's brilliant.

Notes:

[1] objective:目标 例:What is your career objective?（你的事业目标是什么?）

[2] confine:限制,使局限 例:Don't confine your learning only to schoolwork.（不要把你的学习只限制在课堂。）

[3] confused:混乱的,困惑的 例:These issues make parents confused.（这些问题令家长迷茫。）

[4] thesis：命题，论点　例：This is the most problematic part of his thesis.（这是他论题中最有争议的部分。）

[5] element：要素，成分　例：Language is the fundamental element of literature.（语言是文学的第一要素。）

2.3　学以致用（Transference）

1. 请根据下列 Logo，写出相对应的企业中文名称，并指出哪些 Logo 与酒店业相关。

A. _____

B. _____

C. _____

D. _____

E. _____

F. _____

G. _____

2. 选择题

(1) Include all your contact information employers can easily _____ touch with you.

    A. get to   B. get in   C. get up   D. get on

(2) Include resume keywords. That way, you will increase your chances of your resume _____ available positions and of you being selected for an interview.

    A. be match   B. matched   C. have matched   D. matching

(3) There are several basic types of resumes used to _____ job openings.

    A. apply to   B. apply in   C. apply on   D. apply for

(4) _____ your personal circumstances, choose a chronological, a functional, combination, or a targeted resume.

    A. Relying on   B. Standing on   C. Depending on   D. Sitting on

(5) The Equatorial Group of Hotels has _____ itself as a leading operator of hotels in Asia with over 30 years of experience in the hospitality industry.

    A. worked   B. found   C. constructed   D. established

(6) It's always useful to _____ resume templates and samples when you are writing your resume, so you can get an idea of what a resume should (and could) look like.

    A. preview   B. view   C. vision   D. review

3. Listen the following passages, and then fill in the blanks.

When you're a college student or ___(1)___ graduate it can be a challenge to figure out what to ___(2)___ on your resume. However, most college students don't have an ___(3)___ employment history and employers don't expect you to have ___(4)___ work experience.

If you're not sure what to include, do some ___(5)___ about all of your past experiences, including work-related positions, any ___(6)___ you may have done, academic experience, internships, and any awards or special ___(7)___ you may have received. Once you have ___(8)___ a list of all your experience, then you can choose to include ___(9)___ information from your list which pertain to the position you're ___(10)___ for.

4. 模拟实训

要求:四人一组,其中2人作为招聘方列出招聘岗位的具体要求,岗位自拟,另外两人作为面试者针对招聘岗位,制作相应的简历。

2.4 补充英语阅读(Reading)

1. 阅读下列课文并为其找出最合适的标题。

   A. What is a Career Objective?

   B. Where can you Find a Hotel Job?

   C. Why do We Need to Write an Objective for a Hotel Job?

   D. How to Write a Career Objective for a Hotel Job?

2. 阅读下列方框中的职位名称,并从中为课文空白处选出正确的职位。

A. waiter	B. hotel manager	C. housekeeper
D. receptionist	E. cashier	F. concierge
G. accountant	H. tour guide	I. event coordinator

3. 请将课文中的画线部分翻译成中文。

The resume objective is where you want to specify[1] exactly what type of job you are looking for. Your goal is to be as specific as possible so that the rest of your resume focuses on supporting your objective. Many hotel jobs focus on customer service and efficiency, so your objective needs to zero in on[2] how you can contribute[3] these skills to the hotel's business. There are some moderate[4] instructions which are helpful for writing a career objective.

Firstly, read through various hotel job listings to identify the specific requirements and duties of the type of job you want. Pay close attention to the soft skills, such as communication and problem-solving, which the position requires.

Secondly, write a list of your skills and strengths related to the position you are applying for. This will help you create a career objective that clearly states what you have to offer the hotel. For example, if you are applying for a front desk position, communication and customer service skills are vital. A (①) needs to know the local area's nightlife, stores, restaurants, and tourist attractions like the back of his hand, as well as have stellar customer service skills. A (②) should have leadership skills, be able to communicate hotel policies to guests, be able to coordinate and schedule events, be resourceful, and be an on-the-spot problem-solver.

Thirdly, mention how you can help the hotel's business expand[5] or improve, not how you can benefit from working at the hotel. Instead of using phrases like "to understand hospitality better" or "to learn more about hotel management," include phrases like "to enhance[6] the quality of the hotel's event management services" if you are applying for an (③) position, for example.

Fourthly, use the specific job title in the career objective. For example, you may say that you are looking for a position as a hotel security guard, hotel shift manager, housekeeper, concierge, waiter, chef or front desk clerk. Capitalize the title of the position.

Finally, Keep your career objective short. One sentence should do it.

Notes:

[1] specify：具体指定；详细指明；明确说明　例：These documents should specify maintenance responsibility even from the planning and design stages. （这些文件须远在计划及设计楼宇时清楚界定维修责任。）

[2] zeroed in on：向……集中注意力；对准　例：They zeroed in on the suspicious man. （他们的注意力集中在那个可疑分子身上。）

[3] contribute... to：贡献，促成　例：Your suggestion has greatly contributed to the accomplishment of our work. （你的建议大大地促进了我们工作的完成。）

[4] moderate：中等的，适度的　例：The hotel is moderate in its charges. （这家酒店收费适中。）

[5] expand：扩大；扩充；发展　例：He is thinking of expanding his business. （他正考虑扩展他的生意。）

[6] enhance：提高；增加　例：Can we further enhance our competitiveness? （我们能否进一步增强我们的竞争力？）

第三章 英文求职信（Cover Letter）

案例导入（Lead-in）

在求职过程中，很多人会认为相对于简历和各种资格证书而言，求职信可有可无。然而，根据美国知名求职网站 http://www.theladders.com/ 针对求职信的一项统计显示：

1. 83%的求职者会主动向招聘单位提供求职信。
2. 88%的招聘者同意求职信很重要，每个求职者都应该准备一份。
3. 如果没有附一份求职信，39%的招聘者根本不会阅读这份简历。
4. 37%的求职者会根据应聘的不同岗位而撰写不同的求职信。
5. 74%的招聘者会根据求职信中的相关内容向求职者提出面试问题。

问题1　作为一名应届毕业生，你会在求职时主动向招聘单位提供求职信吗？
问题2　你认为求职信和个人简历有什么区别？

3.1　学习焦点（Focus）

在求职过程中，简历是求职程序中的主体，而求职信却可补其不足，起到画龙点睛、锦上添花的作用。因此，求职者可将一些无法在简历中充分展示的个人专长或才能，透过求职信详细说明，从而与简历相得益彰，争取到面试的机会。本章将重点介绍英文求职信的写作方法。

3.1.1 求职信的性质和功能(Function)

求职信也称应征函,在英语中也可称 Application Letter,因其常常置于简历之上,故常被称作 Cover Letter。通常在招聘启事中,用人单位只会要求求职者寄上简历,而求职信则是应聘者为了表达自己对这份工作的热衷而主动提供的材料。换言之,简历是被动的,是个人在求职过程中的必备文件;求职信则是主动的,是求职过程中附带的,其目的就是为了表现出愿望,从而争取面谈机会。

严格来说,一封求职信的文体是正式的。因为写求职信的目的在于争取一份工作,而且阅读求职信的人往往是用人单位的主管领导,所以求职信可被视作一种正式文件。但是,从另一角度来看,是否提供求职信是由求职者本人决定。如果求职者提供了简历而不提供求职信,也不会被认为其求职材料不完整。如果求职者提供了求职信,那是为了强调自己对这份工作的认真态度,属于求职者与受信人之间具有私人性质的额外沟通。那么,融合这两层意义,我们可将求职信视为一种半正式的沟通文件。

求职信的功能就是透过其主动而附带的书写行为和受信者做半正式的沟通,进而使对方了解求职者积极认真的态度,最后达到取得面谈的目的。虽然,简历和求职信的主要功能都在于争取面谈机会,但两者之间也有不同。求职信是简历的附函,是对简历所列的重要经历和能力的强调,使用人单位能更好地注意简历中与职位相关的内容。所以,求职信的内容不必像简历那么完整。

3.1.2 求职信的主要内容(What is involved)

一封完整的求职信主要包括以下四个方面的内容,即 ABCD:

(1) A-aim(写信动机)。通常求职信是针对各大媒体上的招聘广告而写的。求职信中应明确所申请的职位以及求职信息的获取渠道。如果求职者心目中的理想单位并没有公开招聘人才,或者说求职者并不清楚该单位是否有工作机会,也可以通过求职信来毛遂自荐。

(2) B-brief review(个人情况介绍)。在正文中简明扼要地介绍自己,重点是介绍自己与应聘岗位相关的学历水平、经历、成就等,以便让用人单位从一开始就对你产生兴趣。

(3) C-capability and skills（与应聘岗位相符的素质与能力）。这是求职信的核心部分,主要是向用人单位表明自己所具有的专业知识、专业技能、工作经验和成就,以及与本工作要求相符的特长、兴趣、性格和其他相关能力。对于应届毕业生而言,可以略述在学习期间类似的经验。当然,这一部分并不是将简历中的资历再重述一遍,而是有选择性地用资料阐述自己,突出重点,要让对方感到你能胜任这份工作。

(4) D-desire（表示希望得到答复面试的机会）。在信的结尾,最好表示出希望对方给予一次面试的机会,表明自己希望早日成为其中一员的热切心情,并认真地写明自己的详细联系方式。

3.1.3 英文求职信的结构(Essential Parts)

英文求职信一般由七大要素构成:信头、信内地址、称呼、正文、结束礼词、签名和附件。

(1)信头(heading)。信头是求职人的地址、联系方式以及寄信日期。在此,特别强调寄信日期的书写方法。按照美式习惯,日期的顺序为月、日、年的排列,而且日一般用基数词,如"October 11,2011";按照英式习惯,日期的顺序为日、月、年,而且日一般用序数词,如"3rd November,2011"。信头的相关信息必须准确无误,否则,求职人就很有可能收不到招聘单位的回信。在写法上,这点应该注意。有关信头的具体格式将在英文求职信的格式中进行专门介绍。

(2)信内地址(inside addresss)。求职信的信内地址是指收信人的姓名和地址,必须准确、具体。如果求职人对此并不清楚,可以向应聘单位致电问询或通过互联网查询。有关信内地址具体的写作方法将在英文求职信的格式中进行专门介绍。

(3)称呼(salutation)。称呼写在信内地址的下面,与信内地址间隔一行,顶格开始写。在求职信中,称呼一般是 Dear Mr. 或 Dear Ms. 加上收信人的姓(Last Name),之后再打上标点符号,英式用逗号",",美式则用冒号":"。如果求职者实在不清楚收信人的姓名,可用 Dear Director 或 Dear Manager 称呼。如果收信人不是具体的某个人而是机关或者单位,则只写负责人的职位和公司或者机构的名称,如:The Manager, CP Group 或 Jinjiang Hotel 等。

(4)正文(body of the letter)。正文是求职信最重要的部分。正文应在称谓下两行开始,每段文字不宜太长,段落之间应空出一行。正文的开头应说明你申请的职位以及求职信息的来源。通常应聘单位都想知道哪条招聘广告是最为有效的,因此应清楚告知你是在网上,还是报纸,或者其他途径看到招聘信息的。接下来就应写明个人基本情况及优点,并简单地解释为什么这些优点将会成为工作上的优势。值得注意的是,求职者必须将其具备的技能和职位能力要求相关联、相匹配。最后还要指出不能参加面试的时间,并对雇主表示感谢,期望从他们那里得到回复。

(5)结束礼词(complimentary close)。结束礼词相当于我国书信中的"此致"、"敬礼"、"×××敬上"等礼貌用语。其与正文间隔一行,多写于求职信的右端,第一个字母要大写,最后一个词的后面加逗号。结束礼词的表达方式有多种,一般来说其与开头的称呼有着较强的关联,例如:如果求职者知道收件人的姓名,开头的称呼是 Dear Mr. Black,则结束礼词采用 Yours sincerely(英式)或 Sincerely(美式);如果求职者不知道收件人的姓名,开头的称呼是 Dear Sir,则结尾敬辞采用 Yours faithfully(英式)或 Yours truly(美式)。

(6)签名(signature)。结尾礼词的下方应是求职者的亲笔签名。签名的形式虽然是因人而异,但有若干准则必须遵守。最好用钢笔签名,用铅笔、水彩笔或橡皮印盖署的签名,都是很不礼貌的。如果求职信打印的话,务必要在结尾礼词和打印的姓名之间所空的两三行处,亲笔署名,署名时不能加头衔。如果求职者是女性,最好在打印的姓名前注明,以便对方在回信时称呼。如:

Sincerely, 　　　　　此致 敬礼!
(Signature) 　　　　 (亲笔署名)
(Ms.) Wang Xiaoli 　 王小丽(女士)

(7)附件(enclosure)。所谓附件就是指求职者在邮寄求职信时随同附寄的一些能证明个人情况的详细资料。附件通常包括:个人简历、毕业生证书复印件、学位证书复印件、照片、技术资格证书复印件以及个人自传等。如果求职者要在求职信中装入这些材料作为附件,那么,求职者就应当在署名的左下角注明"Enclosure","Encl."或"Encls"。例如:

Enclosure:A resume

Encl. A photocopy of Guide ID Card　　　　附导游证复印件

如果附件材料在两件以上,就应该将"Enclosure","Encl."分别改写成为复数"Enclosures","Encls."。例如：

Enclosures:4 photographs　　　　附上照片 4 张

Encls:5 photocopies　　　　　　　附上复印件 6 份

3.1.4 英文求职信的格式(Layout)

英文求职信的主要内容和中文求职信基本一致,但在格式方面与中文求职信还是有所区别的。其主要表现在信封的写法和信件的格式上。

3.1.4.1 信封的写法(How to Write an Envelope)

绝大多数情况下,外企在华的分支机构或分公司都会在招聘广告中给出中文地址,毕竟要入乡随俗,同时也可以避免邮递员因为看不懂外语而投递困难。在这种情况下,你只需按我国的习惯书写信封即可,只是人名方面须注意。如果广告上写的联系人是中文,那么就直接写"××先生收"、"××女士收";但如果联系人的名字是英文,切记不要擅自把它翻译成中文,哪怕这个名字看起来很普遍、很熟悉。例如："Tom"不要写成"汤姆","Smith"不要写成"史密斯"。

另外一种情况,如果外企给的是英文地址,那信封的写法就应遵循英美的习惯。一般的写法是:在信封的左上角(中文信封邮政编码的地方)写的是发件人的名字和地址,在信封中间的地方写的是收件人的名字和地址。收发双方的地址都要按照由小及大的顺序排列,依次是:第一行写房屋号、门牌号码、街道或路名,第二行写市(县)、省名,第三行写国家名称。需要注意的是,寄往国外的求职信都要加上"中国"字样,邮政编码位于省或者直辖市那行的行尾,而且一定是在国名前。对于发件人来说,如果你留下的是学校班级地址,则一般顺序为:第一行写班级、专业,第二行写系别,第三行写学校(如果系和学校字数少,也可以写在一行),第四行写市(县)、省。你可以每一行后都加上逗号,最后一行句号,也可以行尾不加任何标点符号。此外,名字要写在地址之前。例如：

```
Miss Chen Xue
Department of Tourism and Hospitality          Stamp
Wuhan University              （发信人地址）
16 Luojiashan Road
Wuhan 430072
People's Republic of China



                                      Mr. Simon Smith
                      （收信人地址）Imperial Court Hotel
                                      307 West 79th Street, New York
                                      NY 10023, USA

Personal
```

```
邮编:430072                                                  邮票
武汉大学
陈雪小姐
地址:中国武汉市珞珈山路 16 号


                                  邮编:10023
                                  帝国法院酒店
                                  西门·斯密斯先生
                                  地址:美国纽约州纽约市 79 西街 307 号


私人信件
```

3.1.4.2 信件的格式(Layout of cover letter)

英文求职信常见的格式有三种:缩进式(indented form)、齐头式(block form)和混合式(modified form)。

(1)缩进式。缩进式的求职信,是一种较为传统的信函样式。其信头和日期写在信纸的右上方,且从第二行开始每行向右缩进几个字母,正文每段首行向右缩进几个字母(一般为5个字母),结束礼词和签名写在右下方,附件顶格写。例如:

$$\text{Li Nan}(寄信人:李楠)$$
$$\text{Foreign Language Department}(外语系)$$
$$\text{Fudan University}(上海复旦大学)$$
$$\text{Shanghai } 200052(邮编 200052)$$
$$\text{Sep. } 12, 2011(寄信日期)$$

Mr. Smith(Smith 先生)

Holiday Inn MayFair（巴黎春天假日酒店）

3 Berkeley Street（伯克利街 3 号）

London, W1J 8NE, UK(英国伦敦,地区代号 W1J 8NE)

Tel: 44 - 871 - 9429110

E-mail: Smithsyz@hotmial.com

Dear Mr. Smith: (称呼)

　　I am writing to inquire opportunities for... (应聘原因)

　　During the past four years... (说明能力)

　　Thank you for your consideration... (表示感谢)

$$\text{Yours sincerely,}(结束礼词)$$
$$\text{Li Nan}(手写签名)$$
$$\text{Encl.}(附件)$$

　　(2)齐头式。齐头式是将信头写在信纸的右上角,而将信内地址、称呼、正文、结束礼词、签名、附件的每一行都顶格开始写,段落的开头也不必空格。例如:

$$463 \text{ Guanshan Avenue}(武汉关山大道 463 号)$$
$$\text{Wuhan } 430074(邮编:430074)$$
$$21 \text{ February, } 2010$$

Mr. Li Yun(李云先生收)

6F, Lingnan Hotel(岭南酒店 6 楼)

22 Zhangqian Heng Rd.(广州章谦横路 22 号,邮编:510010)

Guangzhou 510010

Dear Mr. Li Yun:

I am writing to inquire opportunities for...（应聘原因）

During the past four years...（说明能力）

Thank you for your consideration...（表示感谢）

Yours sincerely,（结束礼词）

Wang Peng（手写签名）

Encl.（附件）

(3)混合式。混合式是由齐头式和缩进式混合而成。信头和信内地址用齐头式，而信的正文和结束礼词及签名则用缩进式。例如：

                        Graduate Class（研究生班）

                        Dept. of Tourism（旅游系）

                        Hubei University（湖北大学）

                        Wuhan 430000（武汉 430000）

                        July 9, 2010

Mr. John Brown（John Brown 先生）

Vice President, Human Resource（人事部副部长）

Trans Asia Hotel（Trans Asia 酒店）

283 Huangpu Avenue（黄浦大街 283 号）

Guangzhou, Guangdong 510000（广东广州 510000）

Dear Mr. Smith:（称呼）

    I am writing to inquire opportunities for...（应聘原因）

    During the past four years...（说明能力）

    Thank you for your consideration...（表示感谢）

                          Yours sincerely,（结束礼词）

                          Li Nan（手写签名）

                          Encl.（附件）

3.1.5 英文求职信的常用语句(Useful Expressions)

3.1.5.1 写信动机(Aim)

(1) In reply to your advertisement in today's Hubei Daily, I respectfully offer my services for the situation.

拜读今日《湖北日报》上贵公司的广告,本人特此备函,应征该职位。

(2) Replying to your advertisement in today's issue of the Global Times, I wish to apply for the position in your esteemed firm.

拜读贵公司在今日《环球时报》上刊登的招聘广告,特此备函应征贵公司该职位。

(3) With reference to your advertisement in China Daily of May 25 for the front office manager, I offer myself for this post.

从五月二十五日《中国日报》上广告栏得知贵酒店招聘前厅部经理,本人有意应聘该职位。

(4) I wish to apply for the position advertised in the enclosed clipping from the Hubei Daily of August 5.

谨随函附上八月五日《湖北日报》上贵公司的招聘广告,我愿应聘此职位。

(5) In answer to your advertisement in www.51job.com for a reservationist, I wish to tender my services.

阁下在"前程无忧"网站上刊登招聘预订员广告,本人获悉,特此应聘。

(6) Learning from ×× that you are looking for a sales manager, I should like to apply for the position.

从××处得悉,贵酒店正在招聘一名销售经理,我愿应招此职。

(7) Your advertisement for an operator in the China Daily of May 8 has interested me, I feel I can fill that position.

贵酒店五月八日在《中国日报》上刊登招聘接线员的广告,本人拜读后极感兴趣,相信能担任此职。

3.1.5.2 个人情况介绍(Brief Review)

(1) For the past three years, I have been in the F&B of the Ramada Plaza Optics

Valley Hotel Wuhan, where I have been an head waitress.

本人曾经在武汉光谷华美达酒店餐饮部工作三年,担任餐饮部领班。

(2) I am twenty years of age, and have been employed for the last two years by the May Flower Hotel, in the cashier work of the F&B.

我今年20岁,曾在五月花大酒店服务两年,担任餐饮部的出纳工作。

(3) I am thirty years of age, and am anxious to settle down to office work.

本人30岁,希望能找到一个公司,以便安定下来。

(4) Since my graduation from the college two years ago, I have been employed in Inter Continental Shanghai Puxi as a bellman.

两年前离校后,我在上海浦西洲际酒店担任行李员。

(5) I am currently a student in college. I have over two months more to complete before I graduate. My major is hotel management and I have excellent grades in all my subjects.

我现在是一名大学生,还有两个多月就要毕业了。我主修酒店管理专业,所有课程成绩优秀。

(6) I am twenty seven years of age, female and have two years' experience in the front office of the Shanghai Huatian hotel.

我现在27岁,女性。曾在上海华天酒店前厅部工作两年。

(7) I have been in the business for the last ten years, and worked as the manager in the personnel department.

本人过去10年在公司担任人事部经理。

(8) At school I won a scholarship and the first prize in a speech contest.

在学校,我曾获奖学金及演讲比赛一等奖。

(9) I am a graduate of Hong Kong University, and have in addition an MBA degree from UCLA.

本人毕业于香港大学,并在加州大学获得工商管理硕士学位。

3.1.5.3 个人素质与能力(Capability and Skills)

(1) I have worked for the past three years improving my management knowledge and skills in hotel.

过去三年来，我都在不断提升自己在酒店管理方面的知识和技能。

(2) My college courses have taught me the essential service skills required to contribute to the growth of your hotel.

我在学校所学的课程使我掌握了重要的服务技能，让我能为贵酒店的发展出一份力。

(3) I am able to take dictation in English and translate it rapidly into Chinese.

我会英文的口授笔记，同时能立即将其翻译成中文。

(4) I took the TOFEL in March 2010 and achieved a score of 115, which I hope will be enough to show my English proficiency.

我在2010年3月参加了托福考试并取得了115分的成绩，我希望这足以证明我的英语熟练程度。

(5) I am sure your hotel will be pleased to learn that my English proficiency is excellent. I have excellent skills in both speaking and writing.

我的英文水平不错，说写能力均强，希望能得到贵酒店的赏识。

(6) I have received an English education, and have a slight knowledge of Japanese. I took a Japanese course in college.

本人接受英文教育，同时略通日语。大学时，我修了日语。

(7) In addition to studying the prescribed courses in hotel management, I selected electives such as computer and English courses to help me in my career objective.

我不但修了酒店管理方面的必修课程，而且还选修了计算机和英语等课程，对我的工作能力有很大的帮助。

(8) I believe that my background, experience, and education have given me the unique qualifications for the position.

我相信，凭我的经历、学历和能力，完全能胜任这份工作。

(9) My two degrees and my experience as a sales manager in JW Marriott Phuket Resort & Spa make me the right person, energetic, hardworking and competent for the position you advertised.

我取得了两个学位，在普吉岛万豪度假酒店及水疗中心任过销售部经理，我精力充沛、积极肯干、能力较强，正是你们广告招聘的理想人选。

(10) I could exceed quotas for you every month of the year.

我每月都能超额完成任务。

3.1.5.4 结束语(Closing)

(1) I should be glad to have a personal interview and can furnish references if desired.

如获面试,则感幸甚。如需推荐人,本人也可提出。

(2) I request an interview, and assure you that if appointed, I will do my best to give you satisfaction.

恳请惠予面试之荣。如蒙录用,本人必竭尽所能,为贵公司服务,以符厚望。

(3) I would be grateful for the chance to be interviewed. Please email me at the above address or call me at 88776655.

如蒙惠予面试,我将不胜感激。请按以上地址给我封电邮或拨打88776655。

(4) I have enclosed a resume for your examination. I will be available for an interview any time.

我随函附上了个人简历供您审阅。我随时都能来参加面试。

(5) I am looking forward to discussing with you about the advertised position, and am enclosing a resume for your information.

我希望能和您就广告的职位进一步谈谈。我随函附上了份简历供您审阅。

(6) I would appreciate the opportunity to discuss my qualifications with you in greater detail.

我希望能有机会跟您更加详细地谈谈我的情况。

(7) You will find enclosed an outline of my education and business training and copies of two letters of recommendation.

有关本人的学历、工作经验等项的概要,谨同函呈上两件推荐函。

(8) Enclosed please find a resume and a photo.

随函寄上简历表及相片各一份。

(9) A copy of my transcript is enclosed.

附寄成绩单一份。

(10) Enclosed you will find a letter of recommendation from my former teacher of

English.

随函附上我英文老师的推荐函。

3.1.6 英文求职信实例

Sample 1

Application for a position as an waitress

> Dept. of Tourism
> Hubei University
> Wuhan Hubei (430000)
> May 11, 2011

Mr. Brown(Brown 先生)

Vice President, Human Resource(人事部副部长)

Trans Asia Hotel (Trans Asia 酒店)

283 Huangpu Avenue (黄浦大街 283 号)

Guangzhou, Guangdong 510000 (广东广州 510000)

Dear Mr. Brown:

  I am interested in applying for a position as an waitress at TransAsia Hotel. I found the position advertised at the placement office at Hubei University. I will graduate in June with a degree in hotel management and hope to start my career at that time.

  I am 22, honest, energetic, and good-looking. I have a personality that is cheerful and optimistic. I get along very well with people.

  During my college years, I have worked very hard at my major course so as to lay a solid foundation of theoretical knowledge. As a result, I have passed all the examinations and achieved fairly excellent academic results in major courses such as Hotel English, Theory of Hotel Management, Managing Food and Beverage Operations as well. I also obtained impressive letters of recommendation for my professors.

  I have strong language abilities. I speak Mandarin, Cantonese, and Wuhan dialect. I am highly proficient in both spoken and written English, and I studied Japanese for two years as a second language at college. I can communicate with both English and Japanese Speakers smoothly.

Although my experience as a waitress is limited to my six months of internship with Ramada Plaza Optics Valley Hotel Wuhan, I am familiar with the procedure of service. Last but not least, I am a good communicator, hard working, and enjoy working with people, which make me the title of Excellent Intern.

I enclose my resume, a copy of official transcript and two copies of recommendation letters. I would appreciate it if you can favor me with a prompt reply.

范例一
谋求酒店餐饮服务员一职

广东广州 510000
黄浦大街 283 号
Trans Asia 酒店人事部副部长
Brown 先生

尊敬的 Brown 先生：

我非常希望能在贵酒店谋取餐厅服务员的职位。我是在湖北大学的就业办公室发现贵酒店的招聘广告。我将于今年 6 月份毕业，并取得酒店管理学士学位，然后开始我的工作生涯。

本人现年 22 岁，待人诚恳，精力充沛，容貌姣好。为人乐观豁达，与人相处融洽。

大学期间，我勤奋攻读专业课程，以期打下扎实的理论知识基础，所以我通过了所有的考试并且在诸如酒店英语、酒店管理概论、餐饮部运行与管理等专业课程考试中取得了相当优异的成绩。我的老师还为我写了一封推荐信。

我有很强的语言能力。会说普通话、粤语和武汉方言。我的英语听说能力相当强，而且大学期间我还学过两年的日语。我能流畅地用英语和日语与外宾进行交流。

尽管我做餐厅服务员的经验仅限于在武汉光谷华美达大酒店实习的六个月，

但我对相关的服务程序了如指掌。最后,我还想强调的是,由于我善于交际、工作勤奋且乐于与他人合作,我在实习期间获得了最佳实习生的称号。

随函附寄简历一份、成绩单一份和推荐信两份。如蒙尽早回复,我将不胜感激。

王小丽敬呈
2011 年 5 月 11 日

联系地址:湖北大学旅游系
邮政编码:430000

Sample 2

Application for a position as a hotel manager

18 London Road Forest Hill
London, SE23 3JA U. K.
September 18, 2011

Mr. Smith
Director, Human Resource
Holiday Inn May Fair
3 Berkeley Street
London, W1J 8NE, U. K.

Dear Mr. Smith:

On reading through the Greenville News on September 16, my attention was attracted by your advertisement for a hotel manager. Now as I have a strong desire to obtain such a position, I'd like to apply for the same.

I have broad and diverse experience in the hospitality industry, and my achievements reflect a strong ability to accomplish varied and diversified tasks with regard to the overall management, organizing, planning, and directing of the services in a hotel establishment. I am skilled in the planning of catering, accommodation, and other services; marketing and promotion of the hotel facilities; establishing and achieving profit and sales targets; handling customers comments and complaints; supervising supplies, maintenance, furnishings, and renovations; troubleshooting and addressing problems; recruiting staff and supervising training; and dealing with suppliers and contractors, among others.

I have occupied different work positions: from Front Desk Manager to Sales and Marketing Director, with my present position being Assistant Manager in a 5 star hotel offering 2800 rooms. In the capacity of Assistant Manager, I am responsible for quality control, rooms division, organizing, maintenance and housekeeping activities, communications, and room reservations. I am also an executive committee member involved in the overall policy and budgetary decision making.

I have been working in the field of hospitality management for 12 years and while my current job position is satisfying, the offered position at your hotel represents an opportunity and an ideal next step.

It would be greatly appreciated if you grant me an opportunity of an interview. At that time, I will present my credentials. You can reach me by writing to my above address or contact me at (218) 444-444 at day time.

Yours sincerely,
Peter Wilson

范例二
谋求酒店经理一职

英国伦敦(W1J 8NE)
伯克利街3号
巴黎春天假日酒店人力资源部总监
史密斯先生

尊敬的史密斯先生：

拜读贵酒店在9月16日《格林威尔新闻时报》上刊登的招聘广告获悉贵酒店拟招聘一名酒店经理。现本人急欲寻求这类职位，特此备函应征。

我在酒店行业中有着广博的从业经验。个人成就主要反映出本人在酒店整体管理、组织、计划以及服务指导等方面有着很强的执行能力,能完成多样化和多元化的任务。我在餐饮计划、住宿安排和其他各项服务等方面有着娴熟的技能;精通市场营销,能有效创建和完成销售目标;能妥善处理酒店客户投诉;能很好地监督设备供应、室内设施保养、装修和翻新;能排除故障、应对不同问题;能负责新员工招聘和培训;还能处理与资源供应商、承包商以及其他责任方之间的关系。

本人在酒店业从事过不同的工种:从前厅部经理到销售部总监,再到目前在一家拥有2800间客房的五星级酒店里从事经理助理。作为酒店经理助理,我目前主要负责质量监控、客房部、设备维护和后勤事物、沟通管理以及客房预订等。此外,我还是酒店的行政委员会的成员,参与制定整体政策以及财务预算决策。

我已在酒店管理领域积累了12年的经验。虽然我对目前所从事的工作还比较满意,但是贵酒店所提供的职位能让我有机会在事业中更上一层楼。

如能获面试机会,我将不胜感激。到时,我将面呈证明材料。您可以照以上地址写信给我或在白天打电话与我联系,电话号码是(218)444-444。

彼得·威尔逊敬上
2011年9月18日

联系地址:英国伦敦森林山伦敦路18号
地区代号:SE23 3JA U.K.

3.2 英语情景对话(Dialogue)

3.2.1 What to Include in a Cover Letter

(Liu is talking about the cover letter with Zhang, one of his classmates.)

Liu: I am very confused that why we need a cover letter since we have already fully prepared the resume?

Zhang: Because the cover letter is a very important part of a job application which can initially[1] unveil[2] you as a serious job candidate. And it should always be sent along with your resume.

Liu: I see. That's why most of our classmates are surfing the internet to find the ways to write the cover letter. Can you tell me what is included in a cover letter?

Zhang: When you are writing a cover letter, there is specific information that needs to be included.

Liu: What kind of information?

Zhang: A cover letter should include a contact section, a salutation[3], a body, a closing, and your signature.

Liu: So there are five main parts included.

Zhang: That's right. The most important part of a cover letter is the body of your cover letter. It includes the paragraphs where you explain why you are interested in and qualified for the job for which you are applying.

Liu: So, can I say the cover letter is a good complement[4] for the resume?

Zhang: Yes. But there is one thing you need to remember that a personalized cover letter is always appreciated by the employer.

Liu: It can be time-consuming[5] to write a custom cover letter for each job I apply for.

Zhang: But it's worth it.

Notes:

[1] initially: 最初, 开始　例: The entire wound may not be infected initially. (整个伤口最初可能未被感染。)

[2] unveil: 使公之于众; 揭露　例: The plan was unveiled with the approval from the Minister. (经部长同意该计划被公之于众。)

[3] salutation: 招呼, 致意; 行礼; 问候　例: A deep bow; a muslim form of salutation. (深鞠躬; 穆斯林的一种问候方式。)

[4] complement: 补充物, 补足物; 配对物 [(+to/of)]　例: Homework is a necessary complement to classroom study. (家庭作业是课堂教学的必要补充。)

[5] consuming: 消费的, 消耗(精力或时间)的　例: And it is revealed that white collar community is one of the major luxury consuming groups. (另外, 相关调查显示, 白领阶层是中国奢侈品消费的主要群体之一。)

3.2.2 Some advice for the cover letter

(Liu is consulting Qin, one of his classmates about the cover letter.)

Liu: Qin, would you please read this cover letter I wrote last night? I'd like to have your opinion.

Qin: I'd be glad to tell you what I think.

Liu: If you don't think it's any good, please say so. I really want to get this job.

Qin: Ok, let me see. (After a while) It looks fine to me, but there are still some matters you need to pay attention to.

Liu: Oh, show me please.

Qin: Look at the salutation. You use "Dear Miss". So are sure the lady who will receive your letter is not married?

Liu: Oh, actually I am not sure.

Qin: So, in that case, you'd better use "Dear Madame" instead of it.

Liu: Ok, let me correct it right now.

Qin: Then let's focus on[1] the structure. You know when it comes to the structure of the cover letter four "w" questions should be involved.

Liu: Four "w"? what are they?

Qin: First, what job are you applying for? Second, why do you want to work in this sector and organization[2]? Third, what are you offering? And when are you available for interview?

Liu: Oh, I see. I missed the first W, right?

Qin: Yes. The cover letter should begin with a basic greeting and the position that you are applying for. It should be no more than 2 lines long.

Liu: So in my case if I'd like to apply for the position as a cashier, I need to address it in the first paragraph.

Qin: That's right. But one more thing, if I were you, I would type the letter instead of writing it by hand. It'll look more impressive.

Liu: Good idea. I will type it. Thank you very much.

Qin: Not at all.

Notes:

[1] focus on: (使)集中于　例: The second day of the workshop will focus on the following topics. (工作坊的第二天将集中于下面的主题。)

[2] organization: 组织, 机构, 团体　例: It is a non-profit organization. (这是一个非营利性的组织。)

3.3　学以致用(Transference)

1. 请从下列网站域名中找出招聘求职类的网站。

   (1) www. google. cn

   (2) www. hotresumes. com

   (3) www. yahoo. com. cn

   (4) www. collegerecruiter. com

   (5) www. baidu. com

   (6) www. starwoodhotels. com. cn

   (7) www. careerbuilder. com

   (8) www. monster. com

2. Listen to the following passages, and then fill in the blanks.

   If you want to ___(1)___ your chances of getting a job interview, you should use a ___(2)___ that's written specifically for the person you're addressing and/or the job you're applying for. This means writing a different letter for each and every job vacancy. You should not use ___(3)___ cover letters. These will not be successful and employers can spot them a mile away.

   Remember that this letter is going to be your personal introduction to someone who is ___(4)___ going to be your employer—maybe even your boss. You want to ___(5)___ him or her, in minutes, that you are an ideal candidate for the position and encourage them to learn more about you through reading your resume or CV and (6) you for interview. You'll only do this if you have effectively sold yourself by (7) key skills, achievements and qualities directly relevant to the job.

Most candidates (8) do this. Their cover letters simply mention the advertisement, refer to the attached CV or resume and (9) hope of getting a job interview. But some employers won't even read your resume or CV if your cover letter is poor or (10) so this is a fatal mistake.

Although you'll say more about your (11) in your resume or CV, a good cover letter had the (12) of getting this information in front of your interviewer early on so don't waste the opportunity it gives you to make a great first impression.

3. 请为上述短文选择最合适的标题.

    a. Resume For Job Interview

    b. CV For Job Interview

    c. Application Form For Job Interview

    d. Cover Letter For Job Interview

4. 根据所学内容判断正(T)误(F)。

    (1) The cover letter for resume is very important and should always be sent along with your resume. (　　)

    (2) The cover letter should begin with a basic greeting and the position that you are applying for. It should be more than 3 lines long. (　　)

    (3) The cover letter's purpose is to get the employer to look at the resume. Therefore, if it is written badly, the resume might not get a chance to be looked at. (　　)

    (4) CV is the only way to introduce you and to tell the prospective employer what you can do for them. (　　)

    (5) A cover letter should not be just one page in length. (　　)

    (6) Write the cover letter with the employer's needs in mind, and not your own needs. (　　)

    (7) Each cover letter must be tailored to each job, each employer. (　　)

(8) A cover letter can't serve the same function as the objective statement on your resume(   )

(9) A cover letter tells the employer the type of position you're seeking-and exactly how you are qualified for that position. (   )

(10) The closing of a cover letter should announce an interest in hearing from them soon, and a thank you for their time. (   )

5. Cloze

Take the time to write and __(1)__ your cover letter to fit the employer's requirements as announced in the job advertisement. Be __(2)__ of the __(3)__ for the position and come up with a list of what the employer wants. These requirements are usually included in the job ad and could include the specific areas of __(4)__ the company needs, years of experience of a job applicant, his __(5)__ knowledge, the transferable skills that he possesses, and his __(6)__ traits. You must __(7)__ these items into your cover letter and use it to __(8)__ by example that you have the desired qualifications the company is looking for.

(1) A. personize   B. customize   C. realize   D. fantasize
(2) A. careful   B. prepare   C. aware   D. cautious
(3) A. needs   B. height   C. importance   D. criteria
(4) A. exercise   B. expertise   C. experiment   D. exploration
(5) A. financial   B. potential   C. practical   D. technical
(6) A. emotion   B. personality   C. feature   D. appearance
(7) A. use   B. co-operated   C. incorporate   D. attach
(8) A. explain   B. demonstrate   C. manifest   D. illustrate

6. Choose the right sentences for each cover letter to make them complete.

A

Ms. Rosa Eckard
Pyramid Hotel Group
1705 Zappia Drive
Winchester, KY 40391

Dear Ms. Eckard,

Today, I would like to apply for the Front Desk Agent position at Pyramid Hotel Group. I respectfully include my interested and resume for your consideration.

Thanks so much for posting this opportunity on www.dice.com. I have been seeking a position like this with a prestigious hotel, in which I could apply my extensive and specialized experience to. As an overview, _____(1). I was responsible for _____(2). As this is a smaller hotel, _____(3). This said, I am very conversational, know a lot of about the area and things to do, and have a very positive attitude that I apply to my work.

You will find my qualifications available in more detail in my resume. Please take a look and field any questions you may have to me at (222)-179-7431. Thanks so much for your time, and I hope to hear from you soon.

Sincerely,
Gloria Kerns
Enclosure: resume

B

Dear Mrs. Dickerson,

I am very enthusiastic about the open position I found on www.careerbuilder.com seeking an experienced Waiter for your hotel. Please review my included resume.

I have worked as a Waiter for the past four years at The Richardson. In this time, I have gained _____(1). I am also at present, pursuing a degree in Hospitality Management. I have _____(2). I am _____(3). Above all, I maintain that customer service is the most important task to master as a Waiter.

I look forward to communicating with you further. If you could please call me at (111)-225-8136 to schedule a time to come in, I would very much appreciate it. Thanks for your time.

Sincerely,

Kimbery Campbell

Enclosure: resume

a. I have worked the last seven years as Front Desk Manager for Rosewood Hotels and Resorts

b. a great amount of regulars who come in just to be served by my outstanding Waiter abilities

c. the overall operational and customer service success that the hotel prides itself on

d. considerable experience in what it takes to serve guests in an upscale restaurant environment

e. fast, great at multi-tasking, and can take on many guests at one time

f. I feel that my choice for this Front Desk Agent would be a great start-since you serve more guests

3.4　补充英语阅读（Reading）

1. 阅读下列课文并为其找出最合适的标题。

   A. Why Is Cover Letter so Important

   B. How to Write a Cover Letter

   C. Why We Need To Have a Targeted Cover Letter

   D. Types of Cover Letter

2. 根据课文内容判断正（T）误（F）。

   (1) Employers reduce the pool of cover letters and resumes to a manageable number only by screening their resumes. (   )

   (2) Cover letter is your one opportunity to make a first impression. (   )

   (3) It can be time-consuming when you write cover letter according to the position you apply for. (   )

   (4) When it comes to the Targeted Cover Letters, it's necessary for you to list your skills and experience based on the criteria the employer is looking for. (   )

   (5) The passage is trying to tell us that given this competitive job market, having a generic cover letter is a good choice too, because it can save tons of time for you. (   )

3. 将短文中画线部分翻译成中文。

Employers do manage to reduce the pool of cover letters and resumes to a manageable[1] number. How they do it can give you some insight[2] in to how to write cover letters that will make the cut. Because, if your cover letter doesn't pass muster[3], your resume won't even get a look. If your cover letter and resume aren't perfect they most likely will end up in the reject pile (1). And perfect means perfect-there should not be any typos[4] or grammatical errors. Employers typically won't even consider a candidate that they cannot see is qualified at first glance (2). That first glance at your cover letter is your one opportunity to make a good impression and make it to the next round.

It's certainly easier to write generic[5] or blanket cover letters than it is to write a cover letter specifically targeted to each position you apply for-Targeted Cover Letters (3). However, if you don't invest the time in writing cover letters you're probably not going to get the interview, regardless of your qualifications. This one takes some time and effort and it's not always easy, but, it's important. Take the job posting and list the criteria[6] the employer is looking for, then list the skills and experience you have (4). Either address how your skills match the job in paragraph form or list the criteria and your qualifications.

Given this competitive job market, it is critically[7] important to target your cover letter and your resume. That way the employer knows exactly why you are qualified for the position and why they should consider you for an interview (5).

Notes:

[1] manageable:易办的;可管理的,可控制的 例:This will bring down you monthly payments and hopefully be more manageable. (这将降低你每月付款,并希望更便于管理。)

[2] insight (+into):洞悉,深刻的理解 例:His speech gave us an insight into the problems of education. (他的演讲使我们对教育问题有了深入的了解。)

〔3〕muster:检阅　例:He was abandoned for not passing the muster.（由于没通过检阅,他被遗弃了。）

〔4〕typo:错字　例:Double-check that you have not made any typo, or mistake in copy-pasting.（仔细检查你有没有作出任何错字,或复制粘贴错误。）

〔5〕generic:一般的　例:A generic error has occurred, please contact your administrator.（出现一般性错误,请与管理员联系。）

〔6〕criteria:标准　例:How do we set hiring criteria?（我们如何设定录取标准?）

〔7〕critically:批判性地　例:In the global economy of the 21st century, students will need to understand the basics, but also to think critically, to analyze, and to make inferences.（在21世纪经济全球化中,学生需要学习基础的知识,但同时也要学会批判性地思考、分析和推论。）

求职礼仪篇

第四章 求职形象礼仪（Image and Good Manners）

案例导入（Lead-in）

某五星级国际著名酒店集团以丰厚的条件向社会招聘前厅部工作人员，前来报名的人络绎不绝。其中，有几位女孩认为前台工作代表着酒店的形象，唯有漂亮时尚的人士才会受到酒店的青睐。于是，这几位女孩先到商场购买了名牌服饰，随后又到美容院将自己浓墨重彩地打扮了一番，酷似电视剧里的韩日明星。当她们信心百倍地来到报名地点，谁料人力资源部工作人员连报名的机会都不给她们，就让她们离开现场。看着别的女孩都纷纷报上了名，她们却十分纳闷："这究竟是为什么呢？"

问题1：工作人员为什么不让这几位女孩报名？

问题2：你认为酒店行业对"漂亮"是如何定义的。如果你要去应聘，你会怎么打扮自己？

4.1 学习焦点（Focus）

形象是指能够引起的思想或感情活动的具体形状或姿态，它所反映出的是某个国家、某个产品或者某个个人的整体印象。大学毕业生在求职过程中，对自我形象的塑造是十分必要的。通过恰当的方式和手段，可以在用人单位面前展现出一个鲜活的自我。这种推销自我的方式不仅可以给用人单位留下良好的第一印象，还可以取得用人单位的信任，从而为成功求职增加机会。本章主要从求职着装和仪容修饰两大方面来展开讨论。

4.1.1 求职着装礼仪(Dressing)

着装是对一个人的身份、气质和内在素质的无言的介绍信。它不仅体现着一种社会文化,还体现着一个人的文化修养和审美情趣。因此,从某种意义上说,着装就是一门艺术,它所能传达的情感与意蕴甚至不是用语言所能替代的。在求职场合中,恰当的穿着本身就是一种很好的礼仪。雅致和整洁的服饰具有一种无形的魅力,能让求职者在对方的"第一印象"中留下深刻的记忆。

4.1.1.1 着装礼仪的基本原则(T. P. O. for Dressing)

目前,学者们普遍承认的着装礼仪基本原则就是 T. P. O. 原则。T 指时间(Time),P 指地点(Place),O 指目的(Object)。简言之,着装要与时间、季节相吻合,符合时令;要与所处场合环境,与不同国家、区域、民族的不同习俗相吻合;要根据不同的交往目的、交往对象选择服饰,并符合着装人的身份,力求给人留下良好的印象。

面试是一种正式场合,根据 T. P. O. 原则,衣着应规整得体,修饰自然有度,给人以朴实整洁、合体大方的感觉。为了给自己塑造出良好的着装形象,求职者首先要明确职业特点对职业者服饰的要求,并按这种要求来打扮自己。不同职业,对该职业的劳动者的着装有着特定的要求,只有当求职者的服饰符合职业要求时,才会取得较好的效果。反之,如果不注意这一点,片面地理解美容、着装,忽视职业的特点,很可能会给招聘单位留下不好的印象,求职也难以成功。酒店业是现代社会经济生活中新型服务业形态,其根本出发点就是最大限度地为客人提供满意和愉悦的服务。而服务是依靠人来实施的。因而,酒店服务员的仪容、仪表和仪态都代表着企业的形象,并承载着服务的品质。正是因为这一行业特点,参加酒店业面试的求职人员必须要严格要求自己的着装,树立符合行业标准的职业形象。

4.1.1.2 男士着装礼仪(How to dress as a Man)

(1)西装(Business Suits)。在现代社会的公关社交活动中,人们普遍认为"西装革履"是职业男士的正规服饰。就求职面试而言,穿西装也是最为稳妥和安全的。因此,西装一般成为许多求职者的首选装束。然而,穿西装也有许多讲究,其中最为重要的就是"衣着得体"。体瘦的人,如果穿着深蓝色或中粗竖条的西装,会露出其纤细、瘦弱的缺憾,而穿米色、鼠灰色等暖色调,图案选用格子或人字斜纹的西装,就会显得较为丰满、强壮。瘦高的人,宜穿双排扣或三件套西装,面料选用质感和温暖感觉的,不要选用廓形细窄而锐利的套装。瘦矮的人穿西装时,可用胸袋装饰手帕,为增加胸部的厚度,还可在内袋装入钱包、笔记本等物品。体胖的人可穿深蓝、深灰、深咖啡色等西装,忌米色、银灰等膨胀色,如果是带图案的西装,宜用0.5~2cm的竖条。西装的款型可选用直线型的美国式,这会显得廓形锐利且苗条。值得注意的是,对于应届毕业生而言,应根据自己的经济状况选择价格合理的西装,切忌盲目攀比,乱花钱买高级名牌西服,因为用人单位看到求职者的衣着太过讲究,不符合学生身份,对求职者的第一印象也会打折扣的。

(2)衬衫(Shirts)。男士应选择长袖衬衫,并以白色或浅色为主,因为这样比较容易搭配领带和西裤。平时也应该注意选购一些合身的衬衫,面试前将其熨平整,以免给人"皱巴巴"的感觉。崭新的衬衣穿上去会显得不自然,太抢眼,以至于削弱了人事主管对求职者其他方面的注意。从质地上来说,天然织物是衬衫最理想的布料。求职者应尽可能选择那些经过精心缝制、专业洗涤、中度上浆(挺括)的全棉衬衫。

(3)领带(Ties)。男士参加面试时一定要在衬衣外打领带,且领带宽度多为8~9厘米,领带的下端在皮带上下缘之间为最佳。从质地来看,纯真丝的领带或50%的羊毛和50%的真丝混合织成的领带是面试时的最佳选择。领带上面不能有油污,也不能皱巴巴。此外,选择领带的颜色也颇有讲究,总体来说应与西服颜色相衬,且不能与西服的图案有任何冲突。领带与西装色彩搭配的基本原则:银灰色、乳白西服配红领带,红色、紫色西服配乳白领带,深蓝、墨绿西服配黄、玫瑰领带,褐色、深绿西服配天蓝色领带。黑色、棕色的西服,适宜佩戴银灰色、乳白色、蓝色、白红条纹或蓝黑条纹的领带,这样会显得更加庄重大方。

(4)皮鞋(Shoes)。参加面试时,皮鞋应以黑色为宜,且面试前一天要擦亮。系鞋带的皮鞋是最保守的选择,但如果选择无带的皮鞋,需朴素大方,且鞋帮要浅。

(5)袜子(Men's socks)。袜子的颜色应当和西服相配。通常以蓝、黑、深灰或深棕色为宜,但不要穿颜色鲜亮或花格袜子。袜子要够长,以使求职者在叠起双腿时不至露出有毛的皮肤,以免有失雅观。

(6)公文包(A Brief Case)。求职者在参加面试时,可选择简单细长的公文包,以存放自己的求职材料。但要注意在使用前仔细检查包带或扣是否好使。

（7）首饰（Ornaments）。在面试时，男士可以佩戴结婚戒指和一副小巧柔和的袖扣。除此之外，任何其他的首饰都不妥当。手镯、项链或者纪念章都可能传递错误的信息。

4.1.1.3 女士着装礼仪（How to Dress as a Woman）

女士着装以整洁美观、稳重大方、协调高雅为总原则，服饰色彩、款式、大小应与自身的年龄、气质、肤色、体态、发型和拟聘职业相协调、相一致。

（1）套装（Business Suits）。女士求职服装一般以西装、套裙为宜，这是最通用、最稳妥的着装。不论年龄，一套剪裁合体的西装、套裙和一件配色的衬衣或罩衫外加相配的小饰物，会使女性显得优雅而自信，给对方留下良好的第一印象。女性求职者服装的颜色可有多种选择，一般以黑色或深色套装为主，以凸显自身的成熟稳重。但这也不是千篇一律的。现在社会已逐渐接受一些较鲜艳的颜色，类似谋求公关、文秘类职位的女性就可以选择黄色套装，因为黄色通常表现出丰富的幻想力和追求自我满足的心理。而红色有时也会是一种不错的选择，它能显示人的个性好动而外向，主观意识较为强烈而且有较强的表现欲望，这种颜色感染力强，容易打动面试考官，令其振奋，从而给人深刻的印象，但太过浓烈的红色也会使人有排斥的情绪。粉红色应该是职场女性应该避开的颜色，因其往往给人以轻浮、圆滑、虚荣的印象。

（2）鞋子（Shoes）。与整体着装相协调是女士穿鞋的总原则。面试时，女士选择的鞋子在颜色上和款式上应与服装相配，不要穿长而尖的高跟鞋，中跟鞋是最佳的选择。因为中跟鞋既结实又能体现职业女性的风度。从款式来讲，除皮鞋之外，设计新颖的靴子也会显得自信而得体，但穿靴子时，应该注意裙子的下摆要长于靴端。在夏季最好不宜穿露出脚趾的凉鞋，更不能将脚指甲涂抹成红色或其他颜色。

（3）袜子（silk stockings）。女士在面试时应穿着丝袜，但袜子不能有脱丝，否则有失雅观。通常情况下，肉色丝袜是最适合的选择。为保险起见，女士应在包里放一双备用，以免脱丝能及时更换。

（4）首饰（Ornaments）。戴首饰的重要原则是"少则美"。耳环应当小巧且不引人注目；项链应朴实无华，切忌戴假珍珠或华丽的人造珠宝；若佩戴手镯，应避免镯子上的小饰物,以及其他刻在镯子上的名字。

(5)皮包(A Brief Case)。面试时可选择单肩包或手提包,但应与装面试材料的公文包区别开来。可以只拿公文包而不背皮包,但不能把公文包里的文件全部塞在皮包里而不带公文包。

(6)手表(A Watch)。面试时不宜佩戴过于花哨的手表,以免给人过于稚气的感觉。面试前应调准时间,以免迟到或延时。

(7)眼镜(A Glasses)。在一般情况下,求职者可以佩戴适合自己的眼镜进入面试考场,但由于酒店业非常注重员工的个人形象,尤其是一线服务部门的女性员工因制服和修饰要求不宜佩戴眼镜。因此,若应聘酒店基层服务岗位,则应佩戴隐形眼镜参加面试。

(8)丝巾(A Scarf)。丝巾通常会为女性的美起到画龙点睛的作用,尤其在服务行业中,其已经成为员工制服上不可缺少的一部分。面试时,佩戴一条适合的丝巾会凸显女士的优雅大方。但选择丝巾时一定要注意与衣服协调搭配,如花色丝巾可配素色衣服,而素色丝巾则适合艳丽的服装。

4.1.1.4 求职着装禁忌(Taboos)

无论男士还是女士,在面试时都不能穿T恤、牛仔裤和运动鞋,以免给人随便、不专业的感觉。女士切忌穿太紧、太透和太露的衣服。不要穿超短裙(裤),不要穿领口过低的衣服;夏天,内衣(裤)颜色应与外套协调一致,避免透出颜色和轮廓,否则,会让人感到不庄重、不雅致,也给人轻佻之感,这是求职之大忌。大量的求职实践表明,不论是应聘何种职业,保守的穿着会被视为有潜力的候选人,会比穿着开放的求职者更容易被录用。

4.1.2 仪容修饰礼仪(Grooming)

4.1.2.1 仪容修饰的基本原则(What to Know Before Starting Grooming)

一般来说,仪容主要指人体肩部以上部位(包括发型、面容)和人体未被遮盖的部分。仪容礼仪就是对这些部分进行适当修饰,使其不仅悦目,还与环境和谐,凸显出个体对他人的尊重。

虽然不同功能的社会和不同的交际环境,对仪容修饰有着不同的要求,但仪容礼仪的基本原则是根据自己的年龄、工作性质、职业身份、面容和肤质特征进行美化修饰,以达到整洁大方、无刻意雕琢痕迹、与环境协调的效果。

仪容修饰是整洁仪容的保证。要保持整洁美好的仪容,每天都应该做简单的基础仪容修饰。个体要进行正确有效的仪容基础修饰,一般来说要准备以下基本用品:梳子、吹风、洁面和保湿乳液、爽口水、指甲刀、去脚后跟死皮的软锉等。

4.1.2.2 仪容修饰的一般程序(How to Groom)

仪容修饰并不仅限于面部,而是从头到脚全方位进行的。如果忽略了任何一处的细节,整个仪容修饰的效果就会打折,还很可能会失败。

(1)头发(Hair)。头发清洁,不能有头皮屑和异味。发型应整齐,不应凌乱。除非因工作需要,一般来说男性的头发不宜过长,鬓角不宜过大。女性的发型可长可短,但刘海不宜盖住眉毛。出席正式场合时,头发如染色应力求接近自然,如黑色系列、棕色系列都很适合大多数中国人。一般来说,肤色白皙的头发染色选择度可大一些,女士挑染时加进一些红色往往效果会更好。如肤色暗淡,头发则不宜染色过浅。发型不易怪异。男士不宜佩戴任何发饰,女士如佩戴发饰也以简约、庄重、典雅、大方为主导风格。

(2)眉毛(Eyebrows)。眉型整齐,与五官搭配即可,不要显得刻意修饰。一般来说文眉是禁忌的。如眉毛稀疏或色淡,可用眉笔每天进行涂描。

(3)眼睛(Eyes)。注意保洁,如有分泌物应及时处理。如有眼疾又不得不进行社交活动,应戴墨镜遮掩,以免对方视觉受到不良刺激。

(4)耳朵(Ears)。注意清洁,如耳毛长出耳外应及时修剪。耳环或耳钉不宜过大,以免有张扬之嫌。

(5)鼻子(Nose)。及时清洁,如鼻毛过长要及时修剪。如非特殊职业要求,不要在鼻子上穿挂任何饰物,在别人面前不要擤鼻涕、挖鼻孔。

(6)口腔(Mouth)。牙齿清洁,口腔无异味,与人交往前应忌食气味浓重或刺鼻的食物(如蒜、葱、腐乳,等等),最好先用漱口水,确保去除异味。

(7)嘴唇(Lip)。男性应注意胡须整洁,及时修理;女性如唇上方汗毛过长或颜色过深,应及时清除或漂白。嘴唇应饱满,无裂口或溃疡。天气干燥时,每晚入睡前涂以食用油或蜂蜜有助于保持嘴唇健康,外出前可涂抹无色唇膏。

(8)颈部(Neck)。保持清洁,注意保养颈部肌肤,可定期按摩,并涂抹专用乳霜。

(9)手部(Hands)。保持清洁是最主要的,每次清洁后还应尽可能予以基础护理,如涂抹乳液。如有破损或裂口,要及时处理,以免令他人感到不快或不安。手上有死皮应及时修剪掉。指甲应定期修剪,其长度以不超过指尖为宜。如佩戴首饰,不宜过多。正式场合中(如学术、政务和商务活动),女性如涂抹指甲油,应以红色或粉色系列为宜。

(10)腋毛和腿毛(Armpit Hair and Leg Hair)。女性的腋毛和腿毛如过浓过重,都应采取适当的方式予以脱毛或剃除。

(11)肩背部(Shoulder and Back)。在正式场合,男性不应露肩,上臂也不宜暴露过多。女性则根据具体场合可露肩臂。如选择露肩臂,应确保肩臂干净、无疤痕。

(12)腿部(Legs)。在正式场合中,男性和女性都不应着短裤外装。越是正式的场合,女性的裙子越长。

(13)足部(Feet)。一般来说,正式场合不允许足部直接暴露,但仍要注意足部清洁,确保无异味,定期修剪死皮和脚趾。

(14)其他应注意的问题(Cautions)。面试时,求职者和主考官之间的距离一般不会较远,因此,求职者在参加面试前务必要清除身上的异味,以免影响面试效果。清除异味的方法最常见的有四种。一是在面试前不要吃洋葱和大蒜,也不要喝酒,以免口腔怪味刺人,最好在饭后漱口或刷牙。二是最好在面试前洗个澡,这样既可以把汗臭味冲洗掉,也可以使求职者更加精神抖擞。三是在面试前不要抽烟,烟味会萦绕不散,气味难耐。四是可以在身上适度地抹些香水,香水既可驱散其他气味,又沁人心脾。涂抹香水时,需提前两三个小时,可擦在耳后、衣领处、手肘内侧、手腕、胸前及膝盖内侧,不要把香水直接喷在衣服上。香水的味道应选择清淡型的,如玫瑰香型、米兰型和黄角兰型。

4.1.2.3 面部化妆的基本技巧(How to Make Up)

对于女性求职者而言,为了更好地展示自我魅力,化妆是必要的。它不仅是为了美观,更是体现出求职者对面试官的尊重。但化妆也要讲求适度。求职者应遵循"淡而美"的原则,切不可浓妆艳抹。下面,就针对面部主要部位的化妆技巧进行介绍。

(1)眉毛(Eyebrows)。自古以来,眉毛都是女性的化妆重点。眉形的变化、眉毛的颜色都可塑造出不同的面部感觉。画眉时,首先定好眉峰的位置,用质地稍硬的眉笔从眉毛最浓密的中间部位开始画起,沿眉峰到眼角画出一条流线型的眉毛,并注意眉头处应淡扫。再用刷子轻轻地梳理一下眉毛,使之更加自然、有神。最后不要忘记用化妆棉再将眉毛按几下,将其固定好。眉毛的形状和颜色应与脸形和肤色相称,如脸圆可以把眉毛画立一点,皮肤白可以使用棕色。

(2)眼睛(Eyes)。眼睛是心灵的窗户。因此,眼睛在面试时的作用是举足轻重的。为了使眼睛在面试时能动人而传神,面试之前就应对其稍加修饰。例如,眼睛小的女士可以在眼睛四周轻轻地描上眼圈,但不能描得太黑太深,不要露出修饰的痕迹。单眼皮者也未必一定要去拉双眼皮,有的单眼皮传达出的眼神更坦率、更亲切。如果是近视者,为了不影响美观,可带上隐形眼镜去面试。

(3)鼻子(Nose)。鼻子在整体面部美观度上占有较大的比重。挺拔的鼻梁往往更能凸显个人的气质,也是人们关注的焦点。求职者可以在鼻梁上略施淡粉,以增加其立体感。对于患有粉刺鼻、酒糟鼻和鼻炎者,最好提前到医院去诊治,以免妨碍面谈的效果。

(4)嘴唇(Lips)。嘴唇是面部最富色彩、最生动的地方,也是最吸引人的部分,所以女性求职者应使自己的嘴唇显得有润泽感,以凸显活力。涂口红时,应从上唇着手,先涂唇的内侧,再来是外侧;除了描嘴角外,一直要闭着嘴,否则不一小心口红就会沾在牙齿上。年轻女性在面试场合中宜用紫色口红,避免用大红或橙红,以免给面试官留下刺目的印象。中年人则要与自己深沉的气质相协调,最好选用色调深暗的口红。

4.1.2.4 发型修饰的基本技巧(How to Make Your Hair)

头发是个人仪容中重要的组成部分。按照一般习惯,人们注意、打量其他人,往往是从头部开始的。而头发生长于头顶,位于人体的"制高点",所以更容易先入为主,引起重视。在面试中,清爽干净的头发,再配以适当的发型修饰,无疑能为求职者的形象加分。一般而言,发型修饰应该遵循以下基本原则:

(1)长短适中(Medium Length)。虽然头发的长短是因个人喜好而异,但从社会活动和审美的角度来看,它仍然受到性别、身高、年龄和职业等因素的限制。就职业而言,不同职业对头发长短有一定要求,如服务业对员工头发的长度大都有明确限制:女士头发不宜长过肩部,且工作时应以盘发、束发作为变通;男士不宜留鬓角、发帘,最好不要长于 7 厘米,以免触及衬衫及领口。

(2) 发型得体(Hair Style for Your Own)。选择得体的发型,除了兼顾个人偏好之外,最重要的是要考虑自身条件和社会环境两大因素。

影响发型选择的自身条件主要包括发质、脸形、身高、胖瘦、年纪、性格、着装以及佩饰,等等。而在这诸多的条件中,脸形的影响力最大。选择发型时,一定要遵守应己原则,使二者相互适应。例如,圆脸形的人适宜将头顶部的头发梳高,使脸部视觉拉长;长脸形的人适宜加多脸部两边的头发,使脸部视觉缩短;鹅蛋脸形的人最为标准,适合各种发型;方脸形的人宜在颈部结低发髻,以显优雅;三角脸形的人应增加侧部头发的分量,并用头发稍遮两颊;倒三角脸形的人应将头发往上梳,显得头部稍长;大脸形的人应使头发自然伏贴遮住两颊,以减少脸的宽度;菱形脸的人适合以蓬松的大波浪增加侧面厚度,用头发遮住颧骨,增加脸形的柔和感;国字脸的男士不适合将头发理成板寸。

(3) 美化自然(Not over made-up)。人们在修饰头发时,往往会有意识地运用某些技术手段对其进行美化,这就是所谓美发。一般而言,美发的方法有四种,即烫发、染发、塑发和带假发。对于面试者而言,美发的基本原则就是美观大方,自然得体,忌过分雕琢或是不合时宜。简单的烫发或深色染发都是可行的,而夸张的塑发和戴假发对于求职者而言是不可取的。

4.2　英语情景对话(Dialogues)

4.2.1 Some advice about etiquette of dressing

(Terry is going to attend an interview next week. And now he comes to Mike, his best friend, for some advice.)

Terry: Hi, Mike. I have got the reply from my dream hotel and I'm going to attend the interview next week. Could you give me some advice?

Mike: Definitely. I am so happy for you. First of all, punctuality[1] is the basic rule. Those candidates who arrives 5 or 10 minutes after the appointed time aren't welcome by any interviewer.

Terry: Yeah, that's very important.

Mike: It can be very helpful if you visit the place the day before, and look around to see what the employees are wearing. Thus there is no way you can be late.

Terry: I'll try my best to make a good impression on the interviewer. But it's always easier to say something than to do it.

Mike: It's not too difficult to make a good impression. You need to appear well-groomed and professional. Remember avoiding the extremes of a too elaborate[2] or too casual[3] style. This will put you on the same level as other candidates and makes the interviewer focus more on your qualifications.

Terry: But I love casual style. You see, Bill Gates, the founder of Microsoft, looks as powerful in his jeans and T-shirt as in any corporate suit.

Mike: But Bill Gates never works in the hotel. For example, informal[4] clothes as well as torn jeans and dirty shoes convey[5] the impression that you are not serious about the job, or that you may be casual about your work as you are about your clothes.

Terry: How can I dress properly for the interview?

Mike: Generally, in formal situations like interview, men always wear black suits or dark blue suits and also a white shirt. Only in this way can you gain the respect of the interviewer and his confidence in your judgment.

Terry: It seems that "clothes make the man".

Notes:

[1] punctuality:准时 例:The virtues of thrift, hard work, and punctuality(节俭、勤奋、准时三美德)

[2] elaborate:精心制作的;精巧的;详尽的 例:They made elaborate costumes for the play. (他们为这出戏精心制作戏装。)

[3] casual:随便的,漫不经心的 例:He tried to appear casual. (他试图显得随便一点。)

[4] informal:非正式的,随便的 例:a relaxed and quite informal discussion(放

松的、非正式的讨论)

[5] convey:传达 例:Be sure not to convey information using color alone. (请确保不要只用颜色来传达信息。)

4.2.2 How can I dress in the interview?

(Grace is talking with Cathy, her Career Consultant, about her dressing in the interview.)

Cathy: Hello, Grace. That's a beautiful skirt you have on. Where are you going?

Grace: I am going to attend an interview.

Cathy: An interview? What kind of job do you apply for?

Grace: Since my major is international hotel management, I'll apply for Assistant Lobby Manager.

Cathy: Oh. But I think that dress doesn't exactly match the job.

Grace: You are such a liar. You have just said my skirt was beautiful.

Jason: Don't get me wrong. Your skirt is really beautiful, but you are applying for a position in the hospitality industry[1]. You see, your skirt is very short, and your make-up is too thick. What's more, the color of your lipstick[2] doesn't match your skin. As a hotel staff, you should be professional at any times.

Grace: Why is being professional so important in the hospitality industry?

Cathy: Because hospitality jobs demand you constantly[3] present yourself to guests, whether in a restaurant, hotel, resort, spa or other people-heavy setting. Even in the interview you also need to dress professionally in order to get a good opportunity.

Grace: So it is obviously not appropriate for me to wear such a short dress while serving guests.

Cathy: Yes, when you arrive for your interview, employers are already assessing[4] how their guests will perceive[5] you as an ambassador for their operation.

Grace: Then what should I do?

Cathy: Dress comfortably but as your best self. Choose your colors carefully. Neutral tones work well, but black and white also present a professional appearance.

Notes:

[1] hospitality industry:服务业　例:Hopefully, the article could provide relative clear idea and specific action reference for hospitality industry to implement cleaner production. (希望能给服务业实施清洁生产提供较明确的观念和具体行动参考。)

[2] lipstick:口红　例:Lipstick and hair conditioner are cosmetics. (口红和护发素都是化妆品。)

[3] constantly:不断地;时常地　例:She is constantly changing her mind. (她经常改变主意。)

[4] assess:对……进行估价,评价　例:It is too early to assess the effects of the new legislation. (现在来评价新法规的效果为时尚早。)

[5] perceive:感觉,意识,看待　例:If students perceive themselves as receiving care from teachers and peers, it will also discourage bullying behaviors. (当学生意识到他们受到老师和同辈们的关怀,同样可以减少欺凌的行为。)

4.3　学以致用(Transference)

1. Look at the following dressing pictures and pick up the ones not appropriate for a job interview.

(1)　　　　　(2)　　　　　(3)　　　　　(4)

  (5)   (6)   (7)   (8)

2. Read the text and fill in the blanks with the following words.

Make-up	Tattoos	Nail	Hair
Shoes	Heels and toes	button	Perfume

Personal Grooming

  Your personal grooming standards go hand in hand with your job interview attire: whether the job interview dress code is formal or casual, the following grooming rules should be adhered to:

— __(1)__ freshly washed and neat.

— __(2)__ should be worn but stay neutral.

— __(3)__ should be clean and neat, avoid bright colours and acrylics. Normally the classic colors of natural pink, french manicured or a classic red would be better.

— __(4)__ should be worn sparingly.

— __(5)__ should be polished.

— __(6)__ have been repaired.

— No missing __(7)__ , no lint and no fluff on any clothing.

— __(8)__ should be covered.

— Use a breath mint before you enter the interview.

3. Listen to the following passages, and then fill in the blanks.

  Have you heard that clothes make the woman? Be __(1)__ in your dressing at all times according to the company's level of "professional appearance". The professional image of a company is __(2)__ on your professional dress. The way you dress __(3)__ to everyone around you, your __(4)__, coworkers and boss. It says how you feel about yourself and how you want them to feel about you. Whatever you do must reflect your professional status. Personal __(5)__ is the first step of dress etiquette and to dress elegant. That means a clean and clear face, with make up applied __(6)__ if you need it. Your hair should be __(7)__. Nails should be clean and __(8)__. If you are not __(9)__ with long nails, I suggest you keep them short and __(10)__ looking.

4. Complete the following dialogues.

Dialogue A

Scene: Two students are talking about the interview attire.

Student A: Hi, B. What a beautiful dress you have on. Where __(1)__?

Student B: I am going to attend an interview.

Student A: What kind of job __(2)__?

Student B: You know I am majored in __(3)__, so I apply for a head waitress.

Student A: Oh. Though your dress is so nice, it __(4)__ the job.

Student B: __(5)__?

Student A: Because your skirt is too __(6)__, and your make-up is too __(7)__. As a hotel staff, you should be __(8)__ at any times, interview included.

Student B: So how can I do?

Student A: Just need __(9)__ your dress. __(10)__ must be suitalbe.

Student B: Yes, I have got a black one in my wardrobe. It that all right?

Student A: Great!

Dialogue B

Scene: Student A is asking for some advice about the interview attire.

Student A: Hi, B. I am going to attend a job interview tomorrow morning, so would you give me __(1)__.

Student B: Congratulations on you. __(2)__ and tie would be the best choice.

Student A: Oh, yes. But I don't know (3) I should choose for them?

Student B: Generally, in formal situations, such as interview, men always wear black suits or dark blue suits, and also white (4) .

Student A: Oh I see. And (5) is suitable for me?

Student B: The color is very important. Tell me what color do you like?

Student A: (6) is my favorite.

Student B: Oh, no. Red is not fit for interview. Because it (7) power. So how about a lighter color one?

Student A: Is this light blue one all right?

Student B: That's (8) .

Student A: Thank you.

4.4 补充英语阅读(Reading)

1. 阅读下列课文并为其找出最合适的标题。

   A. Men's Interview Attire

   B. What Is Improper to Wear on an Interview

   C. How to Dress for an Interview

   D. Interview Tips

2. 将文中画线部分翻译成中文。

The first impression you make on a potential[1] employer is the most important one. The first judgment an interviewer makes is going to be based on how you look and what you are wearing. (1) That's why it's always important to dress professionally for a job interview, even if the work environment is casual. What's the appropriate[2] dress code for an interview? You'll want that first impression to be not just a good one, but, a great one. The candidate dressed in a suit and tie is going to make a much better impression than the candidate dressed in scruffy[3] jeans and a T-shirt(2).

Here are some instructions on how to dress for an interview:

Firstly, let's take a close look at the Men's Interview Attire[4]

— Suit (solid color-navy or dark grey)

— Long sleeve shirt (white or coordinated with the suit)

— Belt

— Tie

— Dark socks, conservative leather shoes

— Little or no jewelry

— Neat, professional hairstyle

— Limit the aftershave

— Neatly trimmed[5] nails

— Portfolio or briefcase

Secondly, let's pay attention to the Women's Interview Attire

Suit (navy, black or dark grey)

— The suit skirt should be long enough so you can sit down comfortably

— Coordinated[6] blouse

— Conservative shoes

— Limited jewelry (no dangling earrings or arms full of bracelets)

— No jewelry is better than cheap jewelry

— Professional hairstyle

— Neutral pantyhose

— Light make-up and perfume

— Neatly manicured clean nails

— Portfolio or briefcase

Thirdly, we need to figure out what not to bring to the interview

— Gum

— Cell phone

— Ipod

— Coffee or soda

— If you have lots of piercings, leave some of your rings at home (earrings only, is a good rule)(3).

— Cover tattoos

Finally, let's focus on some interview attire tips.

— <u>Before you even think about going on an interview, make sure you have appropriate interview attire and everything fits correctly</u>(4).

— Get your clothes ready the night before, so you don't have to spend time getting them ready on the day of the interview.

— If your clothes are dry clean only, take them to the cleaners after an interview, so they are ready for next time.

— Polish your shoes.

— <u>Bring a breath mint and use it before you enter the building</u>(5).

Notes:

[1] potential: 潜在的，可能的　例:The dispute has scared away potential investors.（这一争端吓走了潜在的投资者。）

[2] appropriate: 适当的，恰当的，相称的[(+ to/for)]　例:She picked up a dress appropriate for the occasion.（她挑了一件适合该场合穿的衣服。）

[3] scruffy: 肮脏的，衣衫不整的　例:They live in a rather scruffy part of town.（他们住在镇上的肮脏的地段。）

[4] attire: 服装，衣装　例:Do I need formal attire?（我需要穿正式的服装吗?）

[5] trim: 修剪　例:I had my hair trimmed.（我头发修剪过了。）

[6] coordinated: 协调的　例:The plastic color assortment is not very coordinated.（塑料件的颜色搭配不很协调。）

第五章 面试礼仪（Job Interview Etiquette）

案例导入（Lead-in）

某国际五星级大酒店在 A 校园发布广告，需招聘一名经理助理。许多毕业生都准备了厚厚的求职材料以及推荐信，欣然前往应聘。经过紧张的角逐，该酒店经理最终录用了一位没有任何推荐信的小伙子。这一结果引起了其他同学的质疑："凭什么选他，他的成绩又不是最好的，而且连封推荐信都没有？"对此，酒店经理笑着说道："那位同学其实带来了许多推荐信啊。他神态清爽，服饰整洁；进门前在门口蹭掉了脚下带的土，进门后又随手轻轻地关上了门；当他看见残疾人时主动让座；进了办公室，其他人都从我故意放在地板上的书上迈过去，而他却很自然地俯身将书捡起并放回桌上；当我给同学们分发酒店宣传册时，所有学生都坐在那里用单手接过来，只有他站起身，用双手接过这份材料；面对问题时，他回答得简洁明了，干脆果断。你们说这些难道不是最好的推荐信吗？"

问题1　经理话中的"推荐信"指的是什么？

问题2　这位被录取的男同学在面试中遵守了哪些礼仪规范？

5.1　学习焦点（Focus）

求职面试礼仪是求职者在求职面试过程中与招聘单位的接待者接触时应具备的礼貌行为和仪表形态规范。它一般是通过求职者的仪容、仪态、仪表和语言等方面体现其内在修养和素质。作为求职者，都希望在面试时给主考官留下一个良好的印象,从而增大录取的机会。所以,事先了解求职特别是面试的相关礼仪,是求职者迈向成功的第一步。

5.1.1 面试开始时的礼仪(Etiquette on Starting an Interview)

(1)进门时要先敲门(Knocking at the Door Firstly)。在进入面试室时,即使门是虚掩的,也要先敲门,以表示对主考官的尊重。敲门时应用右手背手指关节轻敲门三下,并注意声音大小和速率。经过允许后方可轻轻推门进入,进门时要表现得自然,不要紧张或慌张,进入后再转身轻轻将门关好。

(2)礼貌问候(Greeting)。求职者进入面试现场后,应主动微笑向考官点头致意,礼貌地问候"您好!"或者"大家好!"如果面试考官先向求职者发出问候,则应该视具体情况予以礼貌回应。否则,会是非常失礼的表现。

(3)入座有讲究(Taking Your Seat Properly)。进入面试室后应在面试官指定的位置就座,并经面试官同意后方可入座。入座时应把握"左进左出"的原则,即从左侧走向自己的座位,并从左侧离开自己的坐位,同时要尽量做到无声无息。落座时,应只坐到椅子的 2/3;两脚自然落地,女士双腿双脚并拢,男士双腿可以张开,但不要超过肩宽;双手不要抱胸,不要乱摆,自然地放在膝盖上;挺胸抬头,上身保持端正,切勿左右摇摆,不要靠椅背。

(4)不可主动握手(Don't Offer Your Hands Firstly)。求职者不应主动与考官握手,除非考官主动伸手。行握手之礼,应由考官先伸手,然后求职者再相迎。拒绝或忽视与考官握手,是一种非常失礼的行为。

(5)关掉通信工具(Turning off Your Cellphone)。在进入面试室之前,求职者应主动将随身携带的手机调至静音或关机状态,以免手机的铃声影响到自身和考官的情绪,同时这也是面试进程中的必备礼仪。

5.1.2 面试进行中的礼仪(Etiquette on Having an Interview)

5.1.2.1 自我介绍礼仪(Self-introduction)

面试交谈一般是从求职者的自我介绍开始。自我介绍是展示自我的重要机会,也是面试中不可缺少的一个环节。虽然用人单位已经看过求职者的相关个人材料,但通过自我介绍可以更多地了解求职者的口才和气质。自我介绍一般很短,两三分钟就够了,但这一环节不仅关乎第一印象,而且还涉及之后的问答,甚至还会影响到面试的成败。因此,求职者在做自我介绍时要坚定自信心,稳定情绪,准确把握自己的特长和优势,并用简短精练的语言流畅地表达出来,当然若能恰当地运用幽默的语句,更易于赢得面试官的欢笑与好感。自我介绍的目的是让面试官对求职者有充分的了解,从而判断其是否能胜任所应聘的职位。因此,必须针对应聘岗位重点介绍相关的学历、经历、能力及个性特征,且要言之有物,忌用鉴定式语言勾勒自我,更不可自我炫耀。

5.1.2.2 面试应答礼仪(Responding)

(1)语言简洁得体(Speaking Simply and Appropriately)。话不在多而在精,不要反复强调,生怕考官听不明白或者漏过去,这样反而把重点冲淡了;语言运用要得体,不要说一些"最什么"、"特什么"、"非我不可"等话,让用人单位产生厌恶的感觉。

(2)先问后答(Catching the Whole Question)。求职者必须要让面试官先开口提问,认真听清考官的题目及其要求后,再根据问题的核心做出正确完善的回答,以便和考官取得共识,获得较高的评价。但要把握尺度,忌过分热情,滔滔不绝。

(3)不要打断面试官(Don't Interrupt the Interviewer)。在交谈中,求职者不要打断面试官的说话或抢话头,这种急躁的态度很容易打断或干扰考官说话的思路或误会、曲解考官的意思,是一种非常失礼的行为,会让考官觉得不受尊重。

(4)先思而后言(Thinking before Answering)。对于考官的提问应予以充分重视,绝不能答非所问。如果同时面对几位考官,则应对每一位考官的提问都一视同仁。一般情况下,居中而坐的考官是主考官,求职者应首先回答他提出的问题。当旁边的辅助考官提问时,求职者应适当调整坐姿面向他,以示认真对待。

(5)灵活应变(Be Flexible)。对意想不到的提问必须做出迅速的回答。提出这类问题的目的是考察求职者的应变能力。如果求职者以尴尬的表情无以应对或坐着发呆最容易给考官留下不良印象。应答时应抓住问题的症结所在,边分析边思考对策,做出辩证的回答,即便出现一点小差错,也关系不大。

(6)避免与考官发生冲突(Never Conflicting with the Interviewer)。在与考官的意见不一致时,求职者不要据理力争,以免与考官发生冲突。要知道求职者的生死大权皆掌握在考官手上,即使与考官意见不同,也不能直接给予反驳,可以用诸如:"是的,您说得也有道理,在这一点上您是经验丰富的,不过我也遇到过一件事……"尤其是在下结论时,不要主动说与考官的观点完全相反,要善于引导考官做结论,这样就能避免与其直接发生冲突,同时又巧妙地表明了自己的观点。

5.1.2.3 神态举止礼仪(Proper Manners)

面试是考官与求职者相互交流的过程,其中语言交流只占了30%的比例,眼神交流和面试者的气质、形象、肢体语言占了绝大部分,所以求职者在面试时不仅要注意自己的外表及谈吐,而且要注意神态和举止。

(1)微笑(Smiling)。在面试中,面带微笑,不仅能融洽气氛,增强自信心,而且还可温暖考官的心,引起他对你的注意和好感。

(2)目光接触(Eye-contacting)。求职者应与考官保持目光接触,以表示对其尊重。具体做法为,盯住考官的鼻梁处,每次大约15秒,然后自然地转向其他地方,如望向考官的手、办公桌等其他地方,然后隔30秒左右,又再次望向考官的双眼鼻梁处。切忌目光犹疑,躲避闪烁,这是缺乏自信的表现。

(3)身体姿势和习惯动作(Having Good Posture and Gesture)。在进出面试室时,要注意进退礼仪,保持抬头挺胸的姿态和饱满的精神。与人交谈时,不要频繁地耸肩,手舞足蹈,左顾右盼,坐姿歪斜,晃动双腿等,这些都是不好的肢体语言,总之,手势不宜过多,需要时适度配合表达。

(4)讲话时的嗓音(In a Professional Voice)。嗓音可以体现出一个人是否紧张与自信,因此求职者在平时应多练习演讲、交谈的艺术,控制说话的语速,不要尖声尖气或声细无力,应保持音调平和,音量适中,回答简练,不带"嗯"、"这个"等无关紧要的习惯语,以免显示出在自我表达方面不专业。

(5)留意考官的表情(Be Watching)。求职者还要仔细观察考官的面部表情,并根据其表情变化来及时调整面试内容。当考官对自己的谈话心不在焉时,应立即中止谈论,可采用提问形式引起考官的兴趣,又或者转换话题。

5.1.3 面试结束时的礼仪(Etiquette before Leaving)

在面试结束时,要根据面试结果予以不同的回答,一般而言,有如下几种情况:

(1)当场录用(Be Thankful)。如果求职者当场就告之被录用,切记不要欣喜若狂,得意忘形。首先不忘向考官表达自己诚挚的谢意,并希望在今后的工作中合作愉快。

(2)当场弃用(Staying Calm)。如果未被录用也不必气馁,更不得情绪失控,做出过激行为。求职者应表示从面试中受益匪浅,同时希望今后还有机会与对方做进一步的沟通。但不要用哀求的语气,这样只会让对方感觉到求职者的无能。

(3)结果未定(Be Patient)。如果当场不能知道录用结果,则应再次向考官强调自己对于这份工作的热情和兴趣,并表明自己的决心。同时还要感谢对方能够给予自己这次机会,以及对方能在百忙中抽出时间与自己交谈。

5.1.4 面试结束后的礼仪(Etiquette after an Interview)

面试结束后,求职者一定要耐心地等候消息,不要过早地去打听面试的结果。一般而言,如果在面试两周后或者在考官承诺的通知时间后,还没有收到对方的答复时,就应该写信或者打电话给招聘单位人事部门,询问是否已经做出决定。如果面试失败了,应该保持平和的心态,全身心地投入到第二家面试中,并针对上次面试中的不足,重新做好竞争的准备。

5.1.5 电话面试礼仪(Etiquette on Handling Phone Interview)

某些用人单位在收到简历之后,会采用电话的形式进行首轮面试,以便核实求职者的背景资料和语言表达能力。因此,求职者要想在电话面试中给招聘方留下良好的第一印象,还应具备以下相关的电话礼仪。

(1)环境礼仪(In a Quiet Environment)。求职者应确保电话面试的环境是安静的,以防受到周围环境的干扰,而且还要保证电话信号是畅通的,让双方交流无阻。

(2)准备礼仪(Well Prepared)。电话面试时,最好在手边准备一张纸和一支笔,以备在交谈中做出记录。简历和相关资料应放在正前方,以备面试官提问,同时还应列出一份询问面试官的问题清单,这样就一目了然了。

(3)声音礼仪(Be Heard Clearly)。面对首次电话面试,求职者应努力调整紧张情绪,说话放慢速度,同时确保对方能清楚地听到自己的声音。如果说话太急,容易含混不清,加重紧张情绪。求职者一旦感觉到很紧张,无法继续时,最好向面试官说:"对不起,请让我再来一次,可以吗?"语言谦虚,礼仪得当,才能赢得面试官的好感。

(4)聆听礼仪(Be a Good Listener)。认真聆听是有效沟通的基础,因此求职者应该认真聆听面试官所提出的问题。如果面试官提及专业术语,求职者应做出适当的语音反应,以便让面试官感觉自己的专业熟悉程度。

(5)致谢礼仪(Never Forget a "Thank You for Your Time")。电话面试结束时,求职者应向面试官表示感谢,随后轻轻放下话筒,注意千万不要重重放下,以免引起对方误解,阻碍事情的进展。挂上电话后,求职者可以写一份关于电话面试的简短感谢信,以此来感谢面试官给予这次交谈的机会以及占用他宝贵的时间。另外,如果发现在电话面试中有些重要经历没有提及,那么在感谢信里还可以很好地补充这些附加信息。

5.1.6 求职面试礼仪禁忌(Don'ts for Interview)

对于求职者而言,求职面试的关键就是要尽可能给招聘方留下良好的印象,以增加面试成功的几率。因而,掌握求职面试礼仪是非常必要的。但与此同时,也应该了解一些相关的禁忌,从而为面试做好充分的准备。

(1)缺席或迟到(Never Be Absent or Late)。接到面试通知后,如果不能或不想出席,求职者都应该在前一至三天致电对方,委婉谢绝。恶意缺席不仅是对用人单位的不尊重,同时也会影响到个人声誉,严重地还会影响到个人在此行业中的发展。此外,迟到也是令人无法原谅的行为,直接会给用人单位留下不好的印象。

(2)仪容着装不整洁(Dressing Properly)。无论求职者应聘何种类型的工作,穿着是给他人留下第一印象的机会。邋遢、不修边幅的穿着,不仅是对他人的不尊重,同时也会让人觉得缺乏亲和力和对生活的热情。这种人是不可能受任何单位欢迎的。即便是不穿西服,也至少要把握干净、整洁的原则。

(3)夸夸其谈(Don't Bluff)。在面试中,求职者对自己的经历及能力的表述应该把握实事求是的原则,不要夸大自己的能力,甚至主次不分地"以我为主"。求职者要讲究实在,言简意赅,不可大包大揽地做太多的口头承诺,说得太多了容易引起考官的反感。如果履历表和谈话内容与实际不符,即便面试时未被发觉,日后也会被检验出来,到时候就难以收场了。

(4)言行轻浮(Look and Act Seriously)。考官会通过面试来判断求职者的性格。言行轻浮、行为夸张,会令人有不信任的感觉。求职者如果摆出无所谓、可有可无的态度,那么用人单位也会对其"无所谓"的。另外,在面试中也要把握幽默的分寸,不要将适度幽默与开玩笑混为一谈。随意开玩笑会给考官留下轻浮的印象。

（5）漫天要薪(Don't Ask for an Unreasonable Salary)。在面试中,能进展到与考官谈论薪水这一步,就代表求职者录取的机会较大。但如果不知行情,向考官漫天要价,势必会功亏一篑。因此,求职者在面试前应多渠道打听相关行情,否则就采取"依公司规定"的保守策略。

5.2　英语情景对话(Dialogues)

5.2.1 Some advice about etiquette of interview

(Linda and Lisa are talking about the etiquette of interview.)

Linda: Hi, Lisa, long time no see. I am so happy to see you.

Lisa: Nice to see you again. I heard you are a lobby manager in the very famous Golden Palace hotel.

Linda: Yeah, I'm pretty satisfied with the job right now.

Lisa: That's awesome[1]. Congratulations. What exactly did you do to get you win the interview.

Linda: Focus on the external[2] expressions, because they are important for the first impression. Good manner and style of conversation are always appreciated by the employers. You know, as a potential employee, you need to convince[3] your future boss feel that it is very comfortable to have you around.

Lisa: I see. How can I have the good external expressions?

Linda: Don't worry about that. You need to pay more attention to the details of people's action in life, and you will know how to transfer[4] information by their body language.

Lisa: I'll keep that in mind, but there is another problem. I'm very shy. I guess I may have cold feet when I meet the interviewer.

Linda: Take it easy, Lisa. You need to overcome your nervousness. It is considered an indication[5] that you lack self-confidence.

Lisa: Yeah, you've got the point, but how can I overcome it?

Linda: First, you need to be fully prepared for the interview. Then appear confident. Remember, most people suffer from nervousness in unknown situations. The key is to appear as if you are comfortable. Lastly, take a deep breath before you meet the interviewer, which will help you relax.

Lisa: Ok. I will try my best to overcome it. Is there anything else that I should pay attention to in an interview?

Linda: Yes. Remember don't eat onion or garlic before you go, use a mint before you meet the interviewer.

Lisa: Thank you, Linda. Your advice is very helpful.

Notes:

［1］awesome:令人惊奇的　例:Being a supermodel is awesome.（作为一名超模真是太棒了。）

［2］external:外部的　例:Free from external control and constraint（没有外部的控制和约束。）

［3］convince:说服　例:It is difficult to convince him.（说服他是困难的。）

［4］transfer:转让,转到　例:One of the main forms of technology transfer（技术转让的主要形式之一。）

［5］indication:表明,迹象　例:He gave no indication of his own feeling at all.（他根本没有表明他的感情。）

5.2.2 Responding to a recruitment ad. on telephone

(John is asking Mr. Brown, the hotel manager for some specific information about the positon on telephone.)

Brown: Good Afternoon. Golden Palace, how may I help you?

John: Good Afternoon. May I speak to Mr. Brown?

Brown: May I have your name?

John: My name is John Green.

Brown: Good Afternoon, Mr. Green, this is Tom Brown speaking. What can I do for you?

John: Mr. Green, I wish to apply for the position advertised by your company in last week's Hubei Daily. I am sure that I am competent[1] to meet the requirements that you have specified.

Brown: Well, Mr. Green, can you say something about your qualifications?

John: Of course. I graduated and received a bachelor degree of hotel management from Hubei University in 2009. I have also learned business administration. After graduation, I worked as a lobby manager in Beach Hotel.

Brown: How long have you been working there?

John: Two years.

Brown: Can you tell me something about your job?

John: The main responsibility[2] of my job is to ensure[3] employee and guests welfare as well as assist the organization in improving its quality of service.

Brown: May I ask the reason why you want to leave?

John: I hope to take on new challenges[4] and learn new things with a possible career path.

Brown: I see. Then come in for an interview this Friday morning if it is convenient to you.

John: That's great. Any time is ok?

Brown: How about 9:00 a.m.?

John: No problem. I hope you can give me an opportunity to join your hotel. And I will do my best to prove my value.

Brown: See you on Friday. Good-Bye.

John: Good-Bye.

Notes:

[1] competent:有能力的　例:The nurse was not only competent but also kind. (那个护士不但能干而且亲切。)

[2] responsibility:责任,职责　例:Entrepreneur should afford more responsibility. (企业家需要承担更多的责任。)

［3］ensure:保证　例:Strengthen epidemic prevention and disinfection of animals and ensure health of human and animals.（加强动物防疫消毒,保障人畜健康。）

［4］challenge:挑战,质疑　例:1. This career offers a challenge.（这份职业具有挑战性。)2. Parents are taking legal action to challenge the school's closure.（家长们正诉诸法律反对关闭学校。）

5.3　学以致用(Transference)

1. Listen to the following passage and then fill in the blanks.

Interview Dining Tips

Interviewing can be even more ＿(1)＿ when you are expected to eat and talk at the same time. Dining with a ＿(2)＿ employee allows employers to review your communication and interpersonal skills, as well as your table manners, in a more ＿(3)＿ environment. Table manners do ＿(4)＿. There are some interview dining tips you need to remember:

- Are you really nervous? Check out the restaurant ＿(5)＿ time. That way you'll know exactly what's on the menu, what you might want to order and where the rest rooms are located.

- Be ＿(6)＿. Remember to say "please" and "thank you" to your server as well as to your host.

- Is the table full of utensils? Your salad fork will be on the far ＿(7)＿, your entree fork will be next to it. Your dessert spoon and fork will be ＿(8)＿ your plate.

- ＿(9)＿ are on the right, solids on the left. For example, your water glass will be on the right and your bread plate will be on the left.

- Put your napkin on your lap once everyone is seated.

- Remember to keep your elbows off the table, sit up ＿(10)＿, and don't talk with your mouth full!

2. 下列 ABC 三项中为面试者经常遇到的难题,a－f 是应对难题的小建议,请将其配对。

A. How to Greet the Interviewer

B. How to Respond to Interview Questions

C. How to Close the Interview

a. When you respond to interview questions, listen carefully to the questions, take time to phrase your responses.

b. Towards the end of the interview, let the hiring manager know that you think the job is an excellent fit and that you are very interested in the job.

c. You're selling the interviewer on yourself as the best candidate for the job, so be sure you focus on your relevancy i. e. why you are a good candidate, how you can do the job.

d. When you arrive at a job interview, introduce yourself to the receptionist, if there is one. Let him or her know who you are and who you are scheduled to meet with.

e. It's appropriate to ask what the next step in the hiring process will be and when you might expect to hear.

f. Greet your interviewer with a firm handshake and introduce yourself. Be prepared for a little small talk, but don't overdo it.

3. Read the text and choose the right sentence for each blank.

> a. present a positive personal image
> b. dress accordingly
> c. take note of that handshake
> d. thank them "twice"
> e. be punctual

How to Use Proper Job Interview Etiquette

If your resume has gotten you a job interview, it's just the first big step toward the job you want. When your interview begins, however, job skills become secondary. You're now being interviewed largely on the kind of person you are. Your resume tells people who you are, but your manners — good or bad — show them.

Etiquette is nothing more than the grand set of all good manners. Put simply, etiquette is a language used to relate your respect and consideration to others, like the interviewer, whose opinion matters most. Therefore, the day of your interview is not the time to appear rude, disrespectful or inconsiderate by violating any of the following etiquette tips.

Firstly, __(1)__.

Like anyone at work, your interviewer is in the midst of a busy workday. Show them that their time is valuable to you. Being late tells others that you're self-centered, disorganized, rude or all three. So, leave home with plenty of time.

Secondly, __(2)__.

At an interview, proper etiquette dictates that your manner of dress should by and large fit in with the scene around you, but in a show of respect for the occasion, you should dress just a step above the norm of that environment.

Thirdly, __(3)__.

A firm handshake — in which you pump the hand once or twice with a secure, steady grip, then release — conveys affability and openness, and can create an immediate feeling of comfort between two people.

Fourthly, __(4)__.

During the job interview, countless moments will come up when etiquette is required. Getting them right gives you a confidence visible to your interviewer. Look the interviewer in the eye. Use engaging, non-threatening body language. Good posture alone can convey your interest in being there.

Finally, __(5)__.

At the end of the interview, make sure to thank them both for their time as well as for the opportunity. Don't consider the interview completely over until, that evening, you have written a short thank you note. Keep it short. E-mail is acceptable but snail mail is preferred.

5.4 补充英语阅读(Reading)

1. 阅读下列课文并为其找出最合适的标题。

A. Characteristics of Telephone Interview

B. Score an in-person Meeting

C. Tips for Face to Face Interview

D. Ace Your Telephone Interview

2. 根据课文内容判断正(T)误(F)。

(1) We only need to provide one number is enough, because the interviewer can always find us. (   )

(2) We should study the company's website and the interviewer's background before the telephone interview according to the passage. (   )

(3) If you get passed the telephone interview, that means you are officially hired by the company. (   )

(4) Telephone interview is not very formal, you can take the call wherever you are. (   )

(5) It takes a lot time and energy to weave those background of experience into your conversation. (   )

Do you have a telephone interview coming up? If you are unsure about how to prepare, use these easy tips for preparing and acing your "virtual meeting". Currently, many companies will still start with a phone interview before asking you into the office. And more often than not, this call is with a recruiter that is "screening" candidates before making the decision on who they will bring in. Our four tips could get you one step closer to close the deal.

Tip one: Pick a place to take the call

Many people today take this first interview for granted[1]; they do not schedule time on their calendar and assume that they can take the call anywhere – on the golf course, while driving the kids carpool, or just sitting on the couch. All of these are wrong. Take the call on a landline phone, be in a quiet, familiar location, and stand up and look in the mirror occasionally[2]. We also suggest that you provide two numbers just in case one of the numbers is not working. Be prepared!

Tip two: Know your target

Remember that your interviewer knows you pretty well; they have your resume, or they may have someone on their team that worked with you in a different job. Study the company's website, latest press releases, and job description prior to[3] your phone interview. Get to know the interviewer; study their background just as they have done in preparation for you. Your preparation for this meeting can be reused in the follow-up meetings if this call goes well.

Tip three: Highlight your experience

A great inside tip to use the job description to your ultimate[4] advantage is to highlight all the key words that match your background of experience. Include transferable[5] skills as well. Then weave these exact key words and phrases into your conversation. This requires time, preparation, and planning, so do not try and do this 10 minutes before the call comes in. It's a simple solution with profound[6] results.

Tip four: Be polite

Being polite will serve you well. Try clear, deliberate speaking, and avoid talking over-the-top of your interviewer. Be careful to not talk down or over their head in this situation. The objective of this call is to get you in front of the decision maker! Also show appropriate respect (saying please, thank you, etc.) and make a concentrated effort for balanced dialogue.

Notes:

[1] take for granted:认为……理所当然;(因视作当然而)对……不予以重视
例:You should not take for granted that everyone has the same thoughts as you do. (你不要想当然每个人的想法都和你一样。)

[2] occasionally:偶尔,有时　例:We occasionally meet for a drink after work. (我们下班后偶尔相聚小酌。)

[3] prior to:之前　例:The contract will be signed prior to the ceremony. (合同将在仪式举行之前签字。)

[4] ultimate:①基本的,根本的;最初的,最早的 例:Hard work is the ultimate source of success. (努力工作是成功之本。)

②最终的 例:Independence remains their ultimate political goal. (独立仍是他们最终的政治目标。)

[5] transferable:可转移的,可转让的 例:Any transferable future interest is reachable by creditors. (任何可转让的将来财产权是可被债权人追索的。)

[6] profound:深深的;深刻的;深切的;深度的 例:Her parents' divorce had a profound effect on her life. (她父母的离异对她的生活有很深的影响。)

面试应对篇

第六章　如何包装自我（How to Set up Good Self-image）

案例导入（Lead-in）

求职人：赵静（某旅游院校酒店管理专业，现就职于某五星级国际知名大酒店）

赵静同学刚毕业就就任职于某五星级国际知名大酒店。与其他同学分享成功的面试经验时，她说道：新鲜有趣的故事，比枯燥苍白的自我陈述更能引起面试官的兴趣。如果面试考官记住了你的故事，你就能在众多应聘者中脱颖而出，从而赢得一份 OFFER。我就是一个很好的例子。在面试中，一位主考官让我举一个自认为成功的例子。我马上就联想到自己的实习经历，因为这与面试的职位最为相关。经过迅速整理，我将自己在实习中的工作表现以故事的形式与面试官一同分享。在讲述中，我很注重小细节，尤其是将工作时的情形、心理变化以及神态都活灵活现地描绘出来。没想到我的故事给考官留下了深刻的印象，并帮助我赢得了今天的机会。最后，我总结出一点：把属于你的故事讲好、讲活，就已经成功了一大半。

问题一：赵静同学为什么能在面试中脱颖而出？

问题二：你认为在面试中应如何将故事讲好呢？

6.1　学习焦点（Focus）

在求职面试中，面对众多竞争者，谁能在有限的时间里给面试考官留下最为深刻的印象，谁就更有希望获得工作机会。虽然得体的装扮和良好的仪态确实是一种不错的自我包装，但是在面试交谈中求职者能真正打动考官的心，往往还是靠一个生动有趣的故事或是一个充满智慧的提问。因为讲故事和提问题最能启发人们的思考,它既是一种能深入人心的有效交谈方式,也是能不动声色进行自我展示的一种有效途径。本章内容就围绕在面试中求职者如何用故事包装自我和用提问包装自我这两大方面来展开讨论。

6.1.1 如何用故事包装自我(Be a Good Story-teller)

在求职面试时,求职者用故事情节和细节来描述、表现自我,就是对自我的一种包装。相对于那些苍白无力、让人疑窦丛生的自我表白,一个好的故事会显得更有趣、更新鲜,更能吸引面试官的注意,从而让面试官对求职者有更为直观的了解。这样求职者就更容易获得面试官的信赖,给面试官留下深刻的印象。

6.1.1.1 面试中为什么讲故事(Why Story-telling Is a Good Device?)

在面试过程中,面试官为了判断一个人是否具备所需的才情,通常都会向求职者问一些案例或过往的经验,而这些案例和经验就是故事。例如,某家酒店要招聘一位具有团队合作意识的学生,那么面试考官就会看他在过往参与的事情中有没有表现出团队合作意识。当然,一件事还不能决定一个人,面试官就会继续发问,看三到四个事件中能否找到共同点,就可以判断这个人是否具备这一能力。学生在面试官的追问下回答出的这几个事件,其实就是在讲故事。讲故事不仅能取得面试官更多的信任,同时也能更好地展示自我。

6.1.1.2 面试中的讲述故事的类型(Types of Story-telling)

在面试中,最为常见的叙事方式就是讲述自己在相关专业或行业中所经历的一个案例。例如,在英文面试中,考官会直截了当地向求职者提出这样的问题:"Can you describe a time in your career or job where you had to overcome stress?"或者是"Please tell me a failure that occurred in your job and how you overcame it."等。

第二种方式可能是给出一个开头和结尾、一个词和中心思想,又或者给出几个关键词让求职者讲故事。求职者在允许的范围内可以自由发挥,讲述自己的成长经历,回忆重大事件、成绩与挫折等。

第三种方式是由面试官制造一个环境、氛围,由求职者来设计这种环境下的故事。

6.1.1.3 求职者应在面试中讲什么故事(What to Tell)

每个人都有属于自己的故事,正是这些故事丰富着人们的生活。面试是招聘方和求职方相互沟通、相互了解的过程。对于求职者而言,面试实质上也是讲述故事的另一种形式。通过故事,求职者可以更鲜活地展示出自己优秀的一面,而面试官也可以从求职者的故事中判断出是否需要这样的人才。

在面试中,求职者所讲述的故事可以是发生在身边一件普通的事情,但必须要讲得精彩,且一定要与所应聘的职位密切相关。比如说如何制定策略、如何解决问题、取得什么样的成就、学到什么东西等,这些都能反映出求职者的能力、素质和品质,需要我们在故事中充分挖掘,从而让面试官通过这些故事来感受你的与众不同。

6.1.1.4 如何在面试中将故事讲好(How to Tell)

(1)故事要真实(A True Stroy)。一个好的故事首先要是个真实的故事。如果求职者捏造事实,讲述子虚乌有的事,有经验面试官往往能从细节中发现问题,并且穷追不舍。一旦谎言被拆穿,求职者便会陷入尴尬,并失去面试官对自己的信任。

(2)故事要有针对性(Job-Oriented)。面试时间通常有限,要让面试官在短时间内对你刮目相看,那么你的故事就必须要有针对性。求职者应针对所应聘的岗位,讲最能体现与所求岗位相关的专业技能和优良品质的故事,以故事来展示自我,让面试官觉得你是一位值得信赖的人。在讲述中,求职者不可为了突出自己,而夸大其词,要真正进入到自己的故事中,用真诚来感染他人。

(3)按"STAR(L)"原则讲故事(Basic Principle)。"STAR"原则通常是面试官在与应聘人员交谈时应掌握的基本原则,它是涉及面试实质性内容的谈话程序。对于面试官而言,要判断应聘人员是否符合要求,首先要了解他以前的工作背景,即所谓的背景调查(Situation),然后着重了解该员工具体的工作任务(Task),每一项工作任务都是怎么做的,都采取了哪些行动(Action),所采取行动的结果如何(Result),以及从中学到了什么(Lesson)。

对于求职者而言,如果能遵循"STAR"原则,讲述自己在什么背景下、遇到什么问题或者任务、采取了什么样的手段、得到了什么样的结果,那么求职者的语言既不会累赘,又能切合面试官的倾听流程,让面试官能了解到自己对知识、经验、技能的掌握程度以及工作风格等。由于面试时间短,求职者一定要抓住重点,按照面试官的倾听流程,说出他们想知道的事情,这样就会做到事半功倍。

此外,求职者也可以按照"STAR+L"原则[即"STAR(L)"原则]讲述自己的故事。"L"代表学习,即告诉面试官,你从那个案例中学到什么,假如以后还有类似的机会,你会如何处理;要着重强调自己在故事案例中承担什么角色、做出什么贡献,要凸显自我价值。当然,面试者除了要掌握"STAR(L)"原则讲故事之外,更重要的是要在平时工作中做一位有心人,将自己认为很重要的事情都记录下来,一方面可以从中总结经验、积累素材,另一方面也可以更好地应对面试。

(4)"STAR(L)"原则实例(An Good Example)。英文面试中一个常见的问题是"What is your greatest strength?"下面,是对该问题做出的传统型答案:

My greatest strength is that I am highly organized. I have always been well organized, and have continued to refine this skill throughout my career. I build daily, weekly and monthly plans, and track my performance to these plans so that I stay on tasks and successfully accomplish every proposal I work on.

上述答案虽然较为清晰地阐明了应答者的最大的优势以及如何在工作中发挥这一优势,但由于缺乏具体案例的支撑,显得有些空洞,让人难以信服。如果求职者能将相同的答案按照"STAR(L)"原则来进行展示,那么效果会立竿见影。下面是按照"STAR(L)"原则做出的答案,以供参考。

Intro: My greatest strength is that I am highly organized.

Situation: As a hotel sales manager, one of the most challenging was driving the total hotel revenue from market. When a sales proposal is getting prepared, I had to coordinate the work of the marketing, front desk, food and beverage, housekeeping, engineering, accounting and security departments to ensure a successful sale. Making it even more challenging, we had the goal to get 20% sales increase within half a year.

Task: I knew that being organized was going to be the key to success. I also knew that I would have to communicate with everyone to keep them in the game with me. Additionally, I organized there were some people that could probably give me some great advice.

Actions: To get the proposals done, I first identified the key players I was going to have to work with. I then met with each of them individually to develop their cooperation. I scheduled a meeting with all of them, where we assigned responsibilities, made some rules and time schedule. I used the rules and schedule to hold everyone accountable and communicated with each member, in person and by e-mail, on a daily basis to ensure that everything goes smoothly. This required reviewing every task or detail on the proposals.

Result: My organization skills were critical in keeping everything straight. By communicating with everyone up front and managing the details very closely, we successfully increase the sales by 20%.

Lesson: In addition, I learned from the case that how to handle practical problems with alertness and by optimizing costs. In the future, I am confident that I would do better.

从上述答案中，不难看出采用"STAR（L）"原则来作答，就像讲述故事一样，逻辑性强，且非常注重细节。唯有真实的细节才能打动面试官，给他留下深刻的印象。

6.1.1.5 英文面试前必须准备的六个故事(The Six Stories You Have to Prepare)

良好的准备是成功的保证。要想在面试时将故事讲好，就必须在面试前做好充分的准备。为了应对面试官的提问，求职者需要提前准备一些能展示自己才能的小故事，而这些小故事实质上都是对自我形象的包装。一般而言，面试官通过与求职者的交谈，主要想弄清楚三大问题：一是"你是否会成为企业的财富？"二是"你是否具备团队合作精神？"三是"你是否能适应企业的文化？"

围绕这三大问题，求职者在参加英文面试前通常有六个故事是需要准备的：

(1) The "nature of your challenge" story—Can you articulate what the challenge is that you are trying to overcome? People want to help each other, but they can't and won't unless they can identify with the challenge of others.

(2) The "where you started" story—Are you comfortable talking about the core of who you are and where you started as it relates to what makes you up today?

(3) The "emblematic success" story—Do you have the two to three successes cataloged that emphasize and bring out what makes you uniquely successful?

(4) The "your performance" story—Can you point to and talk about your performance in an objective way that expresses clearly your values and principles for not only what you can do, but how you do it?

(5) The "striving to learn and improve" story—Can you express how you learn from your mistakes and successes and what you are doing to continuously improve?

(6) The "where you are going" story—Can you describe what you want to do, where you want to be in the future, and when you want to get there? Can you describe and tell the story of your dream.

6.1.2 如何用问题包装自我(How to Employ Questions for Image Setting?)

在绝大多数情况下,用人单位在面试进入尾声时会给求职者一个提问的机会,这样做一来是为了给求职者一个直接了解企业的机会,二来是借此进一步对求职者予以考察,因为从提问中可以看出提问者的知识水平、思维方式、个人价值观等。如果求职者能有效利用这样的提问机会来包装自我,不仅会令面试官对其留下良好的印象,同时也是增加面试成功率的砝码之一。因此,问什么问题和怎么问就显得尤为关键。

6.1.2.1 提什么问题(What Questions Should Be Asked?)

The interviewer asks you, "Do you have any questions for me?" You say…"Yes!"这是最简单的面试问题,回答应该是肯定的,否则就相当于放弃了一个表现自己的绝佳机会。作为求职者,究竟应该提些什么样的问题才合适呢? 首先,应提出"表示你对这份工作很有兴趣"的问题;其次,通过提问尽可能地展示出自己对这一职位以及行业的熟悉程度。当然,你所提出的问题和做出的回答都应该强调为什么你是求职者中的最佳人选。

此外,有些问题是求职者不应该在面试环节中主动提出的,例如,薪水、假期或者退休金等相关福利待遇。因为这些问题可能会让你看上去更关心薪金而不是企业本身,尤其对应届毕业生而言。事实上,所有较为规范的企业都会在面试环节中主动向求职者告知福利待遇等方面的规定。如果由求职者主动提问,显然不是明智之举。

第六章 | 如何包装自我(How to Set up Good Self-image)

6.1.2.2 如何提问（Different Questions for Different Interviewers）

虽然求职者在面试中可以提出的问题有很多,但必须要把握"因人而异"的原则,否则一个原本不错的问题可能会成为面试中的一大败笔。所谓"因人而异",就是指求职者在提问前应根据面试官不同的角色类型仔细甄选问题后再来发问。通常根据面试的流程,求职者依次面见的考官会有四大类:人事部主管或经理、部门经理、高层管理者和同事(有可能以旁听身份出现)。下面来看看对这几类角色应提出怎样的问题。

（1）人事部主管或经理(The Recruiter)

人事部主管或经理的主要工作职责就是从众多的求职者中识别出那些具有实力且适合目前职位空缺的人。这一类型的面试官通常可以给求职者一个关于企业的整体构架或对某一部门的总体看法,通过他们的引导,求职者不仅会对招聘方有更深入的了解,而且如果能够成功进入下一轮面试,征求他们的一些建议或了解更多的招聘程序,可以帮助减少在下轮面试中不必要的弯路。适合问这类面试官的问题有:

* How would you describe the company culture? 你怎样形容这家公司的企业文化呢?
* What type of employees tend to excel at this company? 什么类型的员工能在这家公司有比较好的发展?
* Can you tell me more about the interview process? 能给我多讲讲招聘程序吗?
* Could you explain your organizational structure? 你能向我解释一下组织的架构吗?
* What is the company's policy on providing seminars, workshops, and training so employees can keep up their skills or acquire new ones? 为了能让员工与时俱进,公司会有什么样的政策来提供研讨会、专题讨论会和培训呢?

（2）部门经理(The Hiring Manager)

作为求职者,如果最终能得到工作机会,那么面试你的部门经理就很可能是将来管理你的人,因为员工的"处决权"始终会掌握在部门经理的手中,同时部门经理也是对工作职位需求最清楚的人。在面试环节中,求职者可直接向部门经理提出与岗位直接相关的具体问题,比如工作要承担的责任是什么,会遇到怎样的挑战,以及招聘目标是怎样的,等等。如有可能,还可以适时地分析一下自己与他们招聘目标的匹配度,也便于他们更好地了解你的情况。适合问这类面试官的问题有：

* What are the most important skills for the job? 对这份工作来说最重要的能力是什么？
* How would you describe your ideal candidate? 您怎样描述理想中的候选人呢？
* Would you please describe a common career path at the company for someone in this role? 请描述一下公司里做这个职位的人发展前景是什么样的？
* What are the day-to-day responsibilities of this job? 这份工作每天的工作职责有哪些？
* What kind of work can I expect to be doing in the first year? 在第一年里我可以做哪些工作？
* What particular computer equipment and software do you use? 您所使用的计算机设备和软件有哪些？
* How does upper management view the role and importance of this department and this position? 高层管理者是如何看待这个部门的角色和这一职位的重要性呢？
* What do you most enjoy about your work with this company? 在工作中你觉得最有趣的是什么？
* What are the major challenges that you staff is facing right now? 您的员工目前面临最大的挑战是什么？
* What do you consider ideal experience of this position? 您认为应聘这个职位所应具有的最理想的工作经历是什么？

(3) 高层管理者(The Executive /The Industry Expert)

俗话说"站得高,看得远"。企业的高层管理者是对全行业的发展动态最为了解的人,所以具体的工作和行业问题可以从高管那里进行了解。但值得注意的是,求职者的问题应该更多着眼于公司和全行业的发展前途,如果对所应聘职位的行业知识较为了解,不妨借此机会好好展示一下自己,以便能在众多应聘者中脱颖而出。适合问这类面试官的问题有：

* How do you think this industry will change in the next five years? 你觉得这个行业在未来五年会发生什么样的变化？

第六章 | 如何包装自我（How to Set up Good Self-image）

* What do you think gives this company an edge over its competitors? 你觉得公司和其他竞争者相比有什么优势？
* What's the company's biggest challenge? How is it planning to meet that challenge? 公司面临的最大挑战是什么？公司有什么计划迎接这些挑战吗？
* What are the company's strengths and weaknesses compared to its competition? 相对竞争对手而言，公司有哪些优势和弱势？
* Could you describe your company's management style and the type of employee who fits well with it? 您能描述一下贵公司的管理风格以及有哪些类型的员工能充分融入组织？
* How much guidance or assistance is made available to individuals in developing career goals? 公司能为个人在职业发展中提供怎样的引导和帮助呢？
* I read a news story about the possible opening of an office in ×××. Knowing that a news article does not always capture the full story, I wondered what factors are under consideration for this decision. 我从一篇文章中了解到你们准备在×××开一家新店，当然这篇报道的内容有限，我还想了解的是你们在做出这一决定时考虑了哪些因素呢？

（4）同事（The Coworker）

在某些特殊情况下，求职者所面对的面试官中可能会有一位未来的同事，他们往往是以旁听角色出席面试现场的，但在面试过程中你可以主动向他或她发问，因为这样的面试官也许是最坦白与你交流工作的人。如果想了解关于工作中的挑战和工作环境等细节问题，就可以提出你的问题，但别期望了解公司的内部信息，同时还要注意沟通时间不宜过长。适合问这类面试官的问题有：

* What's a typical day like in the department? 在这个部门里最典型的一天是怎么过的？
* How would you describe the work environment at the company? 你觉得公司里的工作环境是什么样的？
* What's the most enjoyable part of your job? What's the most challenging part? 你的工作中最有趣的部分是什么？最有挑战的又是什么？

总之,由于谈话的对象、时间、地点和目的不同,提出问题也应有所不同,切忌千篇一律。求职者要重视提问技巧的学习和运用,方可在面试中把握良机展示自我。

6.2 英语情景对话(Dialogues)

6.2.1 Answering questions is like telling a story

(Ivy is sharing her interview experience with Apple.)

Apple: Hi, Ivy, I heard that you've attended the Accor Hotel Group's job interview, how's going?

Ivy: I can't wait to tell you that, Ivy, I got the job as a receptionist. It really means a whole world to me.

Apple: Congratulations. Ivy. I am so glad to hear that. Your answers must be very brilliant[1]. Can you give me some suggestions on how to handle the interviewer's questions?

Ivy: Sure, first of all, you need to develop a bag of tricks. For example, your story, is the most important aspect[2] of interview preparation.

Apple: So you mean answering questions is like telling a story?

Ivy: Bingo. However, it is impossible to have a story for every possible question you may be asked!

Apple: Then what should I do?

Ivy: You need to select which stories to tell, create a list of what you think your best qualities are.

Apple: What kind of stories can I select?

Ivy: Reflect[3] on accomplishments of your past that demonstrate the qualities you have selected to tell, and organize them into good stories. Remember, details are very important, which can deepen the employers' impression on you.

Apple: I get it. What kind of qualities is the employer seeking for?

Ivy: Well. Such as detail-oriented, calm during a crisis, or a good planner.

Apple: But how can I learn more about what the employer is looking for?

Ivy: You can manage to do that by studying the company's website, reviewing the job description, and talking to people you know at the company.

Apple: I see. Is there anything else I need to pay attention to?

Ivy: Remember, practice telling the stories to a friend or out loud to yourself. You will also find that practicing how to tell a good story is a great confidence-builder, as you are repeating to yourself what your best qualities are! You may also find it helpful to write down one sentence per story on the notepad that you bring into the interview to cue[4] your memory.

Apple: Thank you so much. I will keep that in mind.

Notes:

[1] brilliant:杰出的,优秀的;辉煌的;出色的　例:He came up with a brilliant idea.(他想出了一个绝妙的主意。)

[2] aspect:方面　例:As an important aspect of human culture, funeral and interment culture reflects the level of social civilization.(殡葬文化是人类文化的重要组成部分,它从一个方面反映了社会文明发展的程度和水平。)

[3] reflect:反映　例:Her actions reflect her thought.(她的行为反映她的思想。)

[4] cue:暗示　例:Can you cue me when you want me to begin speaking?(你要我开始讲话时能给我暗示一下吗?)

6.2.2 Don't forget to prepare asking questions

(Michael and Lisa are talking about how to ask questions in the interview.)

Lisa: Hi, Michael, what are you doing now?

Michael: I am preparing for my job interview next week?

Lisa: Oh, great! So how about your preparation?

Michael: I have prepared a lot of questions that will be asked in the interview? Such as "what you like, what you're good at, and what's your working experience" and so on.

Lisa: Is that all?

Michael: You know I have prepared almost 50 questions, which should be enough.

Lisa: Have you prepared some questions to ask the interviewer?

Michael: What? Ask the interviewer? I never think about that.

Lisa: An interview is meant to be a two-way street. The hiring manager is interviewing you to determine whether you're the best fit for the job. At the same time, you should be asking questions to determine whether you would be happy in the position or with the company.

Michael: Oh, you mean both answering and asking are needed in the interview. Is that so?

Lisa: Yes, as a matter of fact, asking is also a great opportunity to set you apart in a positive way from other people being considered for the job.

Michael: So preparing questions to ask is also important to my interview?

Lisa: Of course. Having no questions prepared sends the message that you have no independent thought process, or are ill-prepared, or are not bright, or some combination.

Michael: But I have no idea about how to ask questions. Can you give me some suggestions?

Lisa: Ok. You know interviewers make judgments about you based on the questions you ask. So, you will impress the interviewers if you ask some questions that indicate you've done some good research beforehand[1] and some that demonstrate[2] your interest in working for the company. ?

Michael: How many questions should I ask?

Lisa: There's no set number. It really depends on what you need to know and the time. You may have 20 questions on your mind but there may not be sufficient[3] time allotted[4] to cover them all. So prioritize your questions based on the interview situation.

Michael: Is there anything else I need to pay attention to?

Lisa: Yes. Do not ask questions that are clearly answered on the employer's web site and in any literature provided by the employer to you in advance. What's more, never ask about salary and benefits issues until those subjects are raised by the employer.

Michael: Oh I see. One more thing, when should I ask the questions?

Lisa: In most cases, when you get to the end of the interview, the employer will ask if you have any questions.

Michael: Thank you for your suggestions.

Lisa: Have a good luck.

Notes:

[1] beforehand: 预先　例: We need to make an accurate estimate beforehand. (我们需要事先作出准确的估计。)

[2] demonstrate: 表明, 证明　例: Recent events demonstrate the need of change in policy. (最近的事态表明政策需要改变。)

[3] sufficient: 足够的, 充分的 (+ for/to)　例: Her income is not sufficient to support her family. (她的收入不够养活家人。)

[4] allotted: 拨出的, 指定的　例: Money allotted for payment of such charges. (为支付这笔花费而拨出的钱。)

6.3　学以致用(Transference)

1. 以下是经常出现在面试中的问题, 你认为有哪些问题适宜用讲故事的方式来回答, 请在其方框内用"√"标出。

☐(1) What is your name?

☐(2) What problems have you encountered at work?

☐(3) How many hours do you normally work?

☐(4) How do you handle stress and pressure?

☐ (5) Are you willing to travel on business?

☐ (6) What are you looking for in your next job?

☐ (7) What are your goals for the next five years?

☐ (8) Can you say something about yourself?

☐ (9) What are your salary requirements?

☐ (10) Are you the best person for this job? And why?

2. 假设小强是一名参加面试的应届毕业生,在面试的最后环节中,面试官给机会让小强提问题。下面这些问题中,你认为有哪些是小强不可以向面试官提出的呢？请在其方框内用"√"标出。

☐ (1) How about my salary?

☐ (2) What type of person do you think will be most successful in this position?

☐ (3) How old are you?

☐ (4) Can you say something about the training for new employees?

☐ (5) How much do you earn?

☐ (6) Have you got married?

☐ (7) Did you have a good holiday?

☐ (8) What do you see ahead for your company in the next five years?

☐ (9) What are the career paths in this department?

☐ (10) If you had to convince a friend or colleague to apply for this job, what might you tell them?

3. 阅读下列句子,并将其按正确的顺序排列成一段短文。

A. Know your audience, and make sure you aren't going to offend them or bore them to death.

B. Is your story going to be interesting to the people you plan to share it with?

C. Don't painfully drag your audience down a confusing, thorny path, awkwardly trying to get back on topic afterward.

D. You might want to share the core of your story with someone who has a lot in common with your audience, and listen to feedback.

4. Listen to the following passage, and then fill in the blanks.

第六章 如何包装自我(How to Set up Good Self-image)

Craft the Stories

Think of __(1)__ of your past that can prove the __(2)__ you have selected. The examples should __(3)__ from several of your past jobs, and may also include other areas of your life such as __(4)__ experiences. Think of projects where your role was __(5)__ to the positive result. Do not limit yourself to only __(6)__ experiences, however. Interviewers love to ask __(7)__ questions that invite you to tell them your worst qualities. Include in your bag of __(8)__ a couple of examples about times when things might have ended negatively, but be sure to include a positive __(9)__ about how you __(10)__ the negative experience.

5. Cloze

How to Answer "Tell Me Something about Yourself" in an Interview

When an interviewer asks the dreaded question, "Tell me something about yourself", it can be easy to lose your __(1)__. What exactly does the interviewer want to know? Answering that question can be a breeze. Firstly, keep it __(2)__. The interviewer is not interested in your family, at least not now. Answer the question by emphasizing your best work qualities. Secondly, do not ramble. Keep your answer short and to the __(3)__. It can be easy to lose your nerve and start rambling. Practicing your answer beforehand can __(4)__ a case of the nerves. Thirdly, tell the truth. It can be __(5)__ to lie about your experience and abilities, but honesty counts. Fourthly, talk about your future. Tell the interviewer what your goals are for the future. If your goals __(6)__ growing with the company, mention that. Human resource departments recognize the benefit of hiring individuals who think long term. Finally, mention your __(7)__. Employers want to know that you are aware of your weaknesses. Mention them along with your strong __(8)__ to make a real impression.

(1) A. patient   B. interest   C. passion   D. nerve

(2) A. simple   B. professional   C. complicated   D. interesting

(3) A. text   B. sense   C. point   D. logic

(4) A. highlight   B. maximize   C. minimize   D. eliminate

(5) A. disappointing   B. alluring   C. charming   D. tempting

(6) A. begin   B. accompany   C. involve   D. deal

(7) A. strengths   B. power   C. weaknesses   D. expertise

(8) A. personalities   B. characteristic   C. experience   D. qualities

6.4　补充英语阅读（Reading）

1. 阅读下列课文并为其找出最合适的标题。

   A. Win an Interview by Telling Stories

   B. There Different Ways to Plot Stories about Yourself

   C. Connecting People with Your Stories

   D. How to Make a Good Impression

2. 阅读短文并将下列选项填入文中空白处。

   A. the creativity plot

   B. the challenge plot

   C. the connection plot

When someone says, "So tell me about yourself", a lot of people stumble. When you craft your answer, you have 10 million hours of information to choose from. Many people actually hate getting this question because it's so hard to zero-in on an answer. This is an honest question. Someone wants to know about you. You should learn to choose the right things to say, so you can answer the question in a way that allows people to connect with you and remember you. The best way to have people connect with what you say about yourself, and remember what you say, is to tell a story. Most people instinctively[1] list details about their life, "I did this, then this, then this." It's not very interesting. Stories are more engaging[2], so get used to talking about yourself in stories instead of in lists.

Telling stories about yourself takes practice. A lot of it is trial and error. As you're telling the story out loud, you'll instinctively feel if it's a flop or not. When you find a

第六章 | 如何包装自我（How to Set up Good Self-image）

good story, hone it until you're conveying what you want people to know, in a way they'll enjoy hearing. There are three different kinds of plots we can create about ourselves.

Firstly, ___(1)___. You overcame an obstacle[3] to get to where you are. For example, someone who says, "I'm really good at customer-focused service." It's not very persuasive if someone makes that declaration. But this challenge plot makes things more persuasive: "I learned customer service working at an ice cream stand. In the summer the line was twenty people deep and it was a challenge to keep the customers happy." Now the listener has an image in their mind of you being good at customer service.

Secondly, ___(2)___. In this plot, the turning point in the story is a eureka[4] moment – when an idea comes to you and changes everything. You could say, "My business is about selling textbooks." Or you could say, "I had an idea to sell textbooks, but I couldn't figure out how to market them as interesting to the consumer. Then it hit me that no one has a favorite text book, but everyone has a favorite professor. So I needed to use the professors to hook in the customers."

Thirdly, ___(3)___ This plot comes in when you are telling a story about bringing a team together. For example, "our toy company merged with another toy company and people were duplicating each other's efforts to create a new doll line. I convinced the teams to combine designs and work together. We created a doll that dominated[5] the doll market that Christmas."

Once you've practiced a bit, you can relish[6] the moment someone says, "So, what do you do?" If you understand how to talk about yourself, this is an opening to connect in a meaningful way and make a lasting impression.

Notes:

[1] instinctively: 本能的　例: I felt instinctively that something was wrong.（我本能地感觉到出差错了。）

[2] engaging: 迷人的；可爱的；有魅力的　例: Peter was an engaging young man.（彼得是个可爱的小伙子。）

［3］obstacle:障碍(物);妨碍(+to)　例:His reluctance to compromise is an obstacle to his political success.(他不肯妥协是他政治上成功的一个障碍。)

［4］eureka:感叹词,表示"找到了"

［5］dominate:在……中占主要地位　例:Sports, though important, should not dominate our schools.(运动虽然重要,但不应在学校中占首要地位。)

［6］relish:调味,使……有意味　例:Hunger gives relish to any food.(饥饿使任何食物都具有美味;饥不择食。)

第七章 如何应对面试中的问题（How to Handle the Questions for Interview）

案例导入（Lead-in）

求职人:李萌(某旅游院校酒店管理专业,现就职于某五星级国际知名大酒店)

自述:我是去年12月份获得大堂副理这份职位的。当时与我一同竞争的有200多人,我想我之所以能脱颖而出,关键是沉着自信和灵活应变。在初试中,考官首先要求我们各自做自我介绍。我的自我介绍简短精练,但逻辑性很强,突出个性。当时有一位同学却花了大量的时间在说名字、家里排行等,其实这些都不是重点。在复试中,我独自面对一排面试官,虽然心里有些紧张,但我还是努力表现出自信的一面,因为只有这样才能让自己头脑清醒,灵活应变各类问题。记得当时一位考官问:"你在家是独生女吗?"我知道他这么问的目的是想试探我是否存在娇气、怕吃苦。我微笑着注视着这位考官并回答道:"我有两个哥哥,正是在这种环境中,我养成了一种男孩的性格:豁达、开朗和坚韧。"听罢,考官们立即流露出欣赏的目光。

问题1　你认为李萌在面试中取得成功的原因是什么?

问题2　你认为如何才能回答出令面试官满意的问题呢?

7.1　学习焦点（Focus）

面试是求职过程中的关键,而如何应对面试官的提问则是关键中的关键。面试时间一般较短,除非是国际大型的跨国集团,会有多轮面试,而大多数外企,尤其是酒店,面试一般在2~3轮左右,时间大约在半小时到1小时。在这样短的时间里,求职者要尽量展现自我亮点,给面试官留下不错的印象的确需要技巧。而从面试官的角度来看,要在短时间内真实、全面、准确地了解一个人的个性、能力、综合素质,也是个不小的挑战。本章主要针对英文面试的应对技巧以及面试问题的应答策略来进行讨论。

7.1.1 如何应对英文面试(How to Handle an Interview)

但凡求职者,总会对面试有所担心,而英文面试则是令众多求职者最为头疼的事情。由于面试气氛总是紧张的,人们面对紧张就难免会出错,哪怕说中文都可能会舌头打结,更何况是英文。可俗话说"养兵千日,用兵一时",学了那么多年英语,总会有些积累。如果是因为语言的障碍而错失良机,那的确很可惜。那么,究竟应该如何应对英文面试呢?其实,冰冻三尺,非一日之寒,速成是不可能的。求职者只能在平日积累的基础上,注意一些细节,恰当地运用一些技巧,才可能增加成功的几率。

(1)注重听力训练(Listening Training)。对于立志于在外企工作的人士,平时要十分注重听力训练,至少要在面试时能听得懂考官的提问。如果求职者连考官的提问都听不懂,而反复使用"Pardon",势必给考官留下糟糕的印象,且面试也无法正常进行下去。所以,平时要勤加练习,多听多读,尤其是训练自己对不同国家人说英语的灵敏度,把握其英语发音的特点,以备在面试中能较好地与多国籍的面试官进行交流。

(2)语言流畅(Speak Fluently)。在与面试官用英语交流时,求职者应可能保持流利的语言,且思维要连贯,层次要清晰,切忌在谈话中夹杂着中文。如果面对棘手的问题而不知所措时,千万不要自乱阵脚,可以用"well"、"however"、"this is a good question"这样的过渡词和语句来给自己争取停顿和思考的时间。

(3)表述口语化(Trying to Use Simple English)。有些求职者认为在面试交谈中多使用一些复杂的句型、生僻的单词会让考官认为自己的英语能力很高。其实,这犯了舍本逐末的错误,用简单直白的语言表现最具魅力的自我,才是英文面试的至高境界。不要忽视用"there + be 句型",也不要忽视用第一人称,如果要说某个词却一时想不起来时,那就换种说法,尽量避免卡壳,保持谈话的流畅。

第七章 | 如何应对面试中的问题（How to Handle the Questions for Interview）

（4）回答语速不宜过快（Don't Speak too Fast）。在面试中，有些求职者在听完考官的提问后甚至提问话音还未完全落地，便迫不及待地作答或抢答且语速过快，令在场考官瞠目结舌。其实，这样做很可能会令考官根本没有听懂这种狂飙的中式英语，反而给考官留下浮夸的印象。英文面试的最终目的是要让国外考官了解你，对你感兴趣，而这是需要充分展示自己的综合素质，绝非单一的语言能力。所以，求职者在回答问题时，语速不可过快，应力求表达清晰。

（5）分段式准备（Preparing for each Round of Interviews）。英文面试前应有针对性地分阶段进行准备。以三轮面试准备为例。第一轮面试通常是由人力资源部人员进行，会从求职者的个人简历出发，询问相关的个人问题，比如用英语介绍自己。这一阶段对求职者的英语口语水平要求并不是很高，能熟悉一些日常会话即可。第二轮面试是由部门主管经理出面，重点从个人情况介绍转向专业领域。求职者通常会被要求谈及以往最成功的案例，或者自身的业务强项等。因而，需要熟悉本专业的英语术语，能够用英语与国际专家交流专业问题。第三轮面试，将是对英语口语能力的极大挑战。因为，这轮面试一般是与公司总裁级的人物面对面进行交流，外企的总裁一般是外国人，当然面试也就变成全英语的了。总裁询问的问题一般会和公司的精神、企业文化相关，建议求职者可以在了解企业精神文化的基础上事先准备一份英文底稿并熟记，在交谈时就能比较流畅，但切忌死记硬背，生搬硬套。

7.1.2 英文面试中的十大常见问题及应对策略（How to Handle the Ten Questions）

英文面试时，其实有很多应答技巧和中文面试时并无二致，但往往因为语言不熟练和过度紧张，使得求职者表现失常。下面，就对英文面试中最常出现的十个问题以及应答策略进行分析与总结，以供求职者参考。

（1）"Please tell us something about yourself."能谈谈你自己吗？

◆ 分析：这是个开放性问题，看似简单却不好回答。很多人会滔滔不绝，甚至从自己的出生地讲起，其实这是很没有必要的。考官真正感兴趣的是你的专业背景和你的工作经历。他们之所以这样问其实是在测验你是否能选择重点并且把它清楚、流畅地表达出来。

◆ 对策:有几个基本的方法。一个是直接简要回答所问的问题,另一个是在回答前要求把问题问得更明确。在上述两种情况下,你都要很快地把你的答案转到你的技能、经验和你为得到目前这份工作接受的培训上来。

◆ 范例:I come from a large family and there were a lot of kids to take care of. As a result, I learned efficiency, how to take initiative and could develop very compelling arguments with my older siblings. These skills served me well in my early career as I established myself as a hotel sales supervisor. As I broadened my exposure, this allowed me to take on more demanding roles and complex jobs. For example, I led a project and the project was failing. I always had a knack for solving the most demanding and complex issues that could impact the bottom-line or jeopardize winning a new client. My upbringing taught me not to shy away from difficult situations and that there is always a solution. Together, the attributes would bring tremendous value to your company as you seek to increase sales.

◆ 评语:上述范例只是对个人家庭做了简单的描述后,便很快地将重点话题转到与工作有关的技能和经验上来。而且,回答者是以讲故事的形式来阐述自己的工作经历,令人信服。

(2)"Why should we hire you？"我们为什么要聘用你呢?

◆ 分析:这是个直接、正面的问题,主要是用来考察求职者对岗位和自身优势的认识。

◆ 对策:坦诚和自信是前提条件。求职者在回答时要侧重自身所具备的优势,要让面试官感觉到录用你是对他们而不是对你有利。你需要向他们提供证据以证实你可以帮助他们改进工作效率、降低成本、增加销售、解决问题(如准时上班,改进对顾客的服务、组织一个或多个管理工作等)。

◆ 范例:I sincerely believe that I'm the best person for the job. I realize that there are many other college students who have the ability to do this job. I also have that ability. What's more, I could bring an additional quality that makes me the very best person for the job—my attitude for excellence. Not just giving lip service to excellence, but putting every part of myself into achieving it. In college and at my previous jobs, I worked hard, focused on every details, and always tried to find the

第七章 | 如何应对面试中的问题（How to Handle the Questions for Interview）

best way to deal with issues, which made me become the very best I can become. I think my leadership awards from my college, and my management positions are the result of possessing the qualities you're looking for in an employee.

◆ 评语：在回答中，以实例提供有力的证据，直接而自信地推销自己。

（3）"What is your greatest strength?"你最大的优点是什么？

◆ 分析：这个问题问得非常直接，主要是测试求职者是否具有应聘岗位所需要的素质和技能。

◆ 对策：回答时应当首先强调你已适应的或已具有的技能，因为能否受到雇用在很大程度上取决于这些技能。回答时，一定要简单扼要，重点突出。

◆ 范例：One of my biggest strengths is my communication skills. I work very well with all kinds of people, and understand that everyone has different perspectives about projects and work tasks. So when I work with others I realize that everyone comes to the table with different priorities and objectives. I keep this in mind when I communicate tasks that need to be accomplished with positive reinforcement and awareness of what others are working on.

◆ 评语：范例中先是开门见山地提出了自己的最大优点，然后用工作案例将这一优点进行诠释，重点突出，说服力强。当然，除了"communication skills"之外，还有很多素质和能力可以作为优点呈现，如"love to learn new things"，"well organized"，"a good helper towards those who need it"，"a good team player"，"a quick learner"等。描述这些优点时，都尽可能要提供与工作相关的证据，不然就会显得很空洞。

（4）"What is your greatest weakness?"你最大的缺点是什么？

◆ 分析：这是个棘手的问题。如果求职者照实回答，很可能会失去工作机会。面试官这样问的目的是试图使求职者处于不利的境地，以观察其在类似的工作困境中将作出什么样的反应。

◆ 对策：回答这个问题，可事先针对你所申请的职位特点精心设计好一个答案——即一个"非常切合工作实际，但又可以被容忍和被改正"的缺点。这个缺点跟工作有关、但又不会妨碍你行使工作职责。当然，不论这个缺点是大是小，都不要忘记说明自己是如何在工作中克服这一缺点的。此外，你也可以如实地反映自己目前在工作中存在的不足,但必须能巧妙地用自己的优点去抵消不足,这样也会收到不错的效果。

◆ 范例一:I used to have trouble with procrastinating. Now I have learned to write down a list of things that I need to do, and keep a calendar to keep track of deadlines. I have found that this not only helps me to finish things on time, but it has also helped me to be more organized.

◆ 范例二:Frankly speaking, I do not have much experience with customer service, but I would like to gain experience in this area. I get along well with people, I am able to listen and am a good communicator so I feel that I would get on well in a customer based environment.

◆ 评语:上述两个范例虽然都是在讲述自己的缺点,但却表现了正面的效果。一个完满的回答应该是用简洁正面的介绍抵消反面的问题。

(5)"How has your college experience prepared you for a business career?"你的大学经历为你的职业生涯做好了哪些准备?

◆ 分析:这是应届毕业生们在面试时容易遇到的问题。回答这一问题应注意,当与其他求职者进行比较时,要克服你学习背景中显示出来的任何弱点。

◆ 对策:直接将回答聚焦于自己相对他人而言的优势。

◆ 范例:I have prepared myself to transition into the work force through real-world experience involving internship, travel abroad, and entrepreneurial opportunities. While interning with a private hotel in Hong Kong, I developed a 12-page marketing plan composed in English that recommended more effective ways the hotel could promote its services. I also traveled abroad on two other occasions in which I researched the indigenous culture of the Mayan Indians in Guatemala, and participated in Sino-American Cultural exchange program in Florida. As you can see from my academic, extracurricular, and experiential background, I have unconditionally committed myself to success as a marketing professional.

◆ 评语:回答者明白学习领域与职业领域的不同,因而强调了在大学生涯中参与社会实践的经历,并用事实来支撑自己的优势。

(6)"How would you describe yourself in terms of your ability to work as a member

第七章 | 如何应对面试中的问题（How to Handle the Questions for Interview）

of a team?"你是一名好的团队合作者吗？

◆ 分析：这是酒店面试中常见的问题，因为酒店工作最大的特点就是由团队合作完成。考官通过这个问题来测试你是否能融入组织以及在工作中能否与他人合作完成任务。"个人英雄主义者"往往在面试中是不受欢迎的。

◆ 对策：一个好团队合作者是需要有较强的适应能力、沟通能力和组织能力。请用案例或故事来证明你所具备的这些能力。

◆ 范例：I have had many opportunities in both athletics and academics to develop my skills as a team player. My tenure as a rower with my college's crew team serves as a good example. I learned a great deal about teamwork while rowing because all the rowers in the boat must act as one, which meant that we incessantly worked to keep each movement in the boat synchronized. On an individual basis, we still worked toward group goals through weightlifting and land-rowing. My experience as a marketing research team leader also helped me to learn the role of "team player". I viewed my position as that of group leader and of group member. I ensured that everyone in the group had equal opportunity to contribute, maintained excellent communication among group members, and coordinated their energies toward reaching our team's goal.

◆ 评语：回答者分别讲述了处于人生中两个不同阶段里所发生的案例，强有力地证明了在自己生长经历中是如何扮演好团队合作者这一角色的。

（7）"Why do you want this job?" 你为什么要找这样的职位？

◆ 分析：面试官想借此来了解求职者的工作动机。如果求职者对想从事的工作没有热情或认识不足，那么就不会引起面试官的兴趣。通常，面试官想找那种愿意解决工作中问题的人。他们有理由认为这样的人工作起来会更努力，更有效率。

◆ 对策：要回答这个问题，事先应明确哪些工作适合自身的技能和兴趣。在回答时，要谈及你选择工作目标的动机，而那项工作要求的又是你所具备的技能，各种专业培训，或与职务有关的教育证书。

◆ 范例：I want this job because it is not only a good fit for what I've been interested in throughout my career, but also seems tailored to my competencies, which include communication skill and efficiency. I know, as a receptionist, it requires competence at handling several activities in quick order-customer service, payments, check-in and phones. I like multitasking. As I said earlier, in a previous position, I have a lot of practice in keeping all the balls in the air.

- ◆ 评语:范例中巧妙地运用了"提供证据"技巧,清楚地阐述了自己的工作动机,以及自身能力如何与职位要求相匹配。

(8)"Why did you choose us?"为什么要选择我们公司?

- ◆ 分析:面试官想了解求职者进入公司的动机。唯有热爱这个组织的人,才能在工作中最好地发挥出自己的才干。

- ◆ 对策:"知己知彼,百战不殆"。要表现出对这家公司感兴趣,那首先就必须要了解它。在面谈前,求职者要事先尽可能地对目标企业进行了解。可采用各种媒介,如公司主页、报刊、杂志、宣传册等,甚至是实地察看以获取相关的详细信息。关注公司的年度报告,或任何对你面试有帮助的资料。

- ◆ 范例:I hope to choose your hotel as the beginning of my career because I want to grow. As the saying goes, "well begun is half done". I well understand that your hotel is a famous one in the hospitality industry and boasts a high reputation. And it also offers a lot of opportunities for the employees, such as crossing-training, workplace, seminar. I can not only learn new things, but set a solid foundation for my future career as well.

- ◆ 评语:回答者从公司在行业的美誉度和帮助员工成长的政策这两个方面来阐述自己对该公司的认同和向往。当然,这两个方面是要通过自己对公司的调研才能获得,具有较强的说服力。

(9)"What do you expect to be doing in five years?"你在未来五年内有什么打算?

- ◆ 分析:这个问题是在考察求职者的工作动机。它是在探究求职者是否可以把工作长久地干下去,而且干得努力。

- ◆ 对策:积极正面地回答这个问题才是上策。在回答中应展示自己对工作的热爱和决心,尽可能回避一些负面的情绪。

- ◆ 范例:Although it is hard to predict the future, I sincerely believe that I will become a very good guest service agent. I believe that my abilities will allow me to excel to the point that I can seek other opportunities as a hotel front desk supervisor (the next step) and possibly even higher. My ultimate goal continues to be-and will always be-the best at whatever level I am working at within your organization.

◆ 评语:这是一种可以接受的回答,只是回答太短,也没有提供证据。介绍自己的实例最好放在总结之前。如前台客服专员,需要有强的沟通能力,或者是前台主管有较强的组织协调能力,这些能力都要从自己的实例中体现出来。这样才会使回答变得更加生动。

(10)"Tell me about your salary expectations." 谈谈你对薪水的期望吧。

◆ 分析:如果你对薪酬的要求太低,那显然贬低自己的能力;如果你对薪酬的要求太高,那又会显得你分量过重,公司受用不起。一般情况下,每个职位的薪水事先都会由企业订好预算。他们这么问只不过想证实一下这笔钱是否足以引起你对该工作的兴趣。

◆ 对策:在面试之前必须了解你所在的行业的平均薪水,回答这个问题才能"有底气"。但要注意两点:首先,不要急于作答,也就是说不要主动向面试官挑起这个话题,否则会给人留下"一心只往钱看"的不好印象;第二,作为刚毕业的大学生,作答时不宜说得太多,因为通常新人能"讨价还价"的余地不大。

◆ 范例一:I am looking for my first job, so what I'm more interested is what the position can offer my career.

◆ 评语:对于新人而言,这是一个不错的回答,直接干脆说明自己对工作本身比金钱看得更重要。

◆ I am sure that I am the candidate you are looking for. If you feel the same, I'm sure your offer will be fair and commensurate with the value I can bring the company.

◆ 评语:这是一个很自信的回答,既表达了对公司的信任,同时又流露出对自我工作能力的信任。这不管是对于刚参加工作的毕业生还是对于有过工作经验的人士而言,都会是一个不错的回答。

7.2　英语情景对话(Dialogues)

7.2.1 How to answer tough questions in an interview

(Wang is consulting with Sarah, his Career Consultant, about how to answer tough questions in an interview.)

Wang: Good morning, Sarah. I am going to have an interview next Monday. And I really feel stressful, especially for some tough questions. Can you give me some suggestions?

Sarah: Of course. First, relax. There are no tough questions in an interview, just the ones you haven't prepared for.

Wang: Really?

Sarah: Yes. But you have to apply for the jobs you really want. If you're not, every question will be tough to answer.

Wang: Oh, head waitress is the job I want and I am really sure about that.

Sarah: Great! Then you need to know yourself.

Wang: Knowing myself? What do you mean?

Sarah: Consider your strengths and weaknesses, and be aware of[1] the qualities you offer a potential employer. Think about how your past experiences have helped you.

Wang: Oh, these are really what I need to think about carefully.

Sarah: After doing so, then come the questions. Before the interview, think about or write down all the possible questions you could be asked, and come up with answers to them.

Wang: But how can I figure out[2] all the possible questions?

Sarah: Look over your resume before the interview as many questions may come from your resume. You know what the interviewer wants to know is all about you. Besides, you also can find some good questions from the internet.

第七章 | 如何应对面试中的问题(How to Handle the Questions for Interview)

Wang: If I find the questions, how can I answer them properly?

Sarah: You should recognize that the interviewer is interested in you. So don't sell yourself short, and realize that you have something to offer. This will make questions easier to answer.

Wang: So I need to itemize[3] my skills, values, and interests as well as my strengths and weaknesses. Emphasize[4] what I can do to benefit the company rather than just what I am interested in.

Sarah: Exactly. How smart! Remember; try to answer all questions as positively as you can. Don't speak negatively about former employers, former companies or former management.

Wang: I see. But one more thing, Sarah. If I don't understand the question asked by the interviewer, how can I do?

Sarah: It is alright to ask them to repeat it. Don't assume[5] you can fake your way through an answer.

Wang: Thank you for your advice. These really favor me a lot.

Notes:

[1] be aware of:意识到　例:Many people have started to be aware of the harmfulness of fake commodities.(许多人已开始意识到假冒商品的危害性。)

[2] figure out:弄清楚,理解,算出　例:In an experiment, researchers tried to figure out if this movie fantasy was actually possible.(研究人员在一项实验中,设法理解这样的电影情节是否真有可能发生。)

[3] itemize:详细列举;分条列举　例:Itemize your property damage and, for each item, state the amount or attach an itemized bill or estimate.(详细说明您的财产损失,并逐项列明财产、金额或附上一份详细说明的清单或估价。)

[4] emphasize:强调　例:They wished to emphasize more fundamental issues.(他们希望强调更重要的问题。)

[5] assume:假定　例:You can assume his innocence.(你可以假定他是无辜的。)

7.2.2 Getting a good answer and rehearsing

(Chris is talking with Pam, who is a senior human resource manager in a five star hotel, about how to get a good answer in an interview.)

Chris: Pam, I'm so nervous about my interview next week. I am afraid I get stumbled[1] by the questions being asked. Can you give me some suggestions on how to answer the interviewer's questions properly?

Pam: Well, Chris, relax. Everyone is nervous on interviews. According to my experience, rehearse[2] your answers and time them can be very helpful.

Chris: Oh, I never time my answers before. Why should I do that?

Pam: Because the interviewers don't like rambling[3] answers. Keeping them clear and right to the point, and remember never talk for more than two minutes straight for each questions.

Chris: I get it, I guess I should memorize answers word by word.

Pam: There is no way you can do that. Because it feels like you are faking everything beforehand, which can leave the interviewer a very bad impression on you.

Chris: Then what should I do to get an excellent answer?

Pam: Firstly, don't be afraid to include your own thoughts and word. In order to get a great answer, try to jot down and review a few key words for each answer. And then rehearse your answers frequently, I believe by using this way, it is much better than just memorize answers word by word.

Chris: It sounds good. I will definitely rehearse my answers as much as I can, and hopefully they will come to my mind naturally in interviews.

Pam: Great!

Chris: Is there other suggestion you can give me?

Pam: Well, before you form an answer, you need to figure out what an employer wants most in his or her ideal candidate, then show how well you can meet the qualifications in your answers.

Chris: So that is to say I have to match my abilities with the needs of the employer.

Pam: That's right. The employer is like a buyer. You must find out what the buyer is buying, what he is looking for. Once you know what he wants, you can then present your qualifications as the perfect "key" that fit the "lock" of that position.

Chris: It makes a lot of sense. Thank you, Pam. I really appreciate for you advice.

Notes:

[1] stumbled: 绊脚, 绊倒 (+ on/over)　例: He stumbled on the staircase and hurt his leg. (他在楼梯上绊了一跤, 伤了腿。)

[2] rehearse: 排演, 排练　例: We need to rehearse a new piece of music for the concert. (我们需要为音乐会排练一部新的音乐作品。)

[3] rambling: 散漫, 冗长　例: I really don't want to have to listen to another of his long, rambling speeches. (我真是不想再听他冗长而杂乱的讲演了。)

7.3　学以致用 (Transference)

1. Reading the following passage, and mark "√" in front of the illegal questions.

Federal and state laws prohibit prospective employers from asking certain questions that are not related to the job they are hiring for. Questions should be job-related and not used to find out personal information. Some questions, such as your race, gender, religion, marital status, age, disabilities, ethnic background, country of origin, sexual preferences are illegal. Any one of them is discriminatory.

According to the above passage, which of the following questions is (are) illegal?

☐ (1) What is your name?

☐ (2) How long have you been working there?

☐ (3) How old are you?

☐ (4) How long has your family been in this country?

☐ (5) What is your address?

☐ (6) Why should I hire you?

☐(7) Are you considering having children?

☐(8) Are you a US citizen?

☐(9) Do you have a disability?

☐(10) Does your religion prevent you from working weekends or holidays?

2. 以下列举了面试中常见的问题以及回答问题的思路。请为每个问题找出正确的答题思路。

Questions:

(1) Can you say something about yourself?

(2) What do you think are the most important abilities a receptionist should always have?

(3) What software are you familiar with?

(4) Did you find yourself in really stressing situations in your previous job?

(5) How do you deal with stress and angry clients?

(6) What is your long-range objective?

(7) How has your education prepared you for your career?

(8) Are you a team player?

(9) Have you ever had a conflict with a boss or professor? How was it resolved?

(10) What is your greatest weakness?

How to answer:

A. This is a broad question and you need to focus on the behavioral examples in your educational background which specifically align to the required competencies for the career.

B. Focus your answer on the behavioral process for resolving the conflict and working collaboratively.

C. Talk about what you've done to prepare yourself to be the very best candidate for the position. Use an example or two to back it up.

D. Be honest about this question. Mention what happened and how you would manage different situations in order to overcome the pressure and give the best

第七章 | 如何应对面试中的问题(How to Handle the Questions for Interview)

results to the company.

E. Make a list of the applications you are familiar with before going to the interview and show the interviewer how interested you would be in learning how to use new software.

F. The key is to focus on your achievable objectives and what you are doing to reach those objectives.

G. Almost everyone says yes to this question. But it is not just a yes/no question. You need to emphasize teamwork behavioral examples and focus on your openness to diversity of backgrounds.

H. Talk about a true weakness and show what you are doing to overcome it.

I. Attitude; a receptionist should always have a friendly and polite attitude towards clients and enjoy working and interacting with people.

J. Always mention how easy it is for you to handle difficult situations not getting stressed. The client is always right and there is always a way to find a diplomatic solution to problems by following the company policy and protocol.

3. Choose the best answer for the following interview questions.

Questions:

(1) Why should I hire you?

(2) What is your long-range objective?

(3) Are you a team player?

(4) What is your greatest weakness?

(5) Have you ever had a conflict with a boss or professor? How was it resolved?

Answers:

A. Within five years, I would like to become the very best accountant your hotel has. I want to work toward becoming the expert that others rely upon. And in doing so, I feel I'll be fully prepared to take on any greater responsibilities which might be presented in the long term. For example...

B. I have had trouble in the past with planning and prioritization. However, I'm now taking steps to correct this. For example…

C. I work too much. I just work and work and work, which is my greatest weakness.

D. You should hire me because I'm the best person for the job. I realize that there are likely other candidates who also have the ability to do this job. Yet I bring an additional quality that makes me the best person for the job-my passion for excellence. I am passionately committed to producing truly world class results. For example…

E. Yes, I have had conflicts in the past. Never major ones, but there have been disagreements that needed to be resolved. I've found that when conflict occurs, it helps to fully understand the other persons' perspective, so I take time to listen to their point of view, then I seek to work out a collaborative solution. For example…

F. My education has focused on not only the learning the fundamentals, but also on the practical application of the information learned within those classes. For example…

G. Yes, I'm very much a team player. In fact, I've had opportunities in my work, school and athletics to develop my skills as a team player. For example, on a recent project…

H. I believe she would say I'm a very energetic person, that I'm results oriented and one of the best people she has ever worked with. Actually, I know she would say that, because those are her very words. May I show you her letter of recommendation?

4. Listen to the following passage, and fill in the blanks.

Tell me about yourself

While this query seems like a piece of cake, it is difficult to answer because it is so __(1)__ . The important thing to know is that the interviewer __(2)__ does not want to know about your hometown or what you do on the weekends. He or she is trying to __(3)__ you out __(4)__ . Pick a couple of points about yourself, your professional experience and your career goals and stick to those points. Wrap up your answer by

第七章 | 如何应对面试中的问题(How to Handle the Questions for Interview)

bringing up your desire to be a part of the company. If you have a __(5)__ response prepared for this question, it can lead your conversation in a direction that allows you to elaborate on your __(6)__.

5. Cloze

Does the thought of going on a job interview cause your palms to sweat and your body to break out in hives? Stop itching; you're not alone. The vast __(1)__ of job seekers admit to emotions ranging from __(2)__ uneasiness to downright panic leading up to their interviews. The good news is there have been no reported cases of job seekers who died of nervousness during a job interview. So relax and follow these simple tips for keeping your __(3)__ at bay before and during your interview.

First, take the proper amount of time to prepare for your interview. Being well-prepared will __(4)__ your confidence and lower your anxiety. Experts recommend that you spend at least three hours preparing for each interview.

You should __(5)__ answers to the most common interview questions and practice speaking them out loud. You also should read up on the company with which you will be interviewing and prepare some questions of your own. This lets the interviewer know that you are truly __(6)__ in the company and the position.

As a final step in your preparation, make sure you have good __(7)__ to the interview site. Some job seekers make a dry run to the interview site to ensure the directions are correct and to __(8)__ the amount of time they will need to get to the interview on time.

(1) A. plenty　　　　B. minority　　　　C. majority　　　　D. large
(2) A. strong　　　　B. mild　　　　　　C. weak　　　　　　D. wild
(3) A. satisfaction　　B. scary　　　　　　C. anxiety　　　　　D. happiness
(4) A. weaken　　　 B. bluff　　　　　　C. boost　　　　　　D. eliminate
(5) A. sketch　　　　B. draft　　　　　　C. memorize　　　　D. make up
(6) A. popular　　　 B. interested　　　　C. match　　　　　　D. favor
(7) A. orientation　　B. horizons　　　　C. directions　　　　D. stimulation
(8) A. appraise　　　B. estimate　　　　C. assess　　　　　　D. underestimate

7.4 补充英语阅读(Reading)

1. 阅读短文,将下列选项填入文中适当位置。

    A. Describe a problem situation and how you solved it.

    B. Why do you want to work here?

    C. Why should we hire you?

    D. What accomplishment are you most proud of?

    E. What are your greatest weaknesses?

2. 阅读短文,根据上下文翻译文中画线部分。

How to answer these tricky questions?

Going into a job interview is often like entering the great unknown. Although every interviewer is different and questions vary[1] from industry to industry, there are some questions that are common across the board. Reading through the following questions and developing your own answers is a good place to start in your preparation. Once you have done that, remember practice makes perfect! <u>Nothing impresses a potential employer like being ready for whatever is thrown your way.</u> (1) Here are some suggestions about how to answer these tricky questions.

Here's the chance to really sell yourself. You need to briefly and succinctly[2] lay out your strengths, qualifications and what you can bring to the table. Be careful not to answer this question too generically, however. <u>Nearly everyone says they are hardworking and motivated</u>[3]. <u>Set yourself apart by telling the interviewer about qualities that are unique to you.</u> (2)

This is one tool interviewers use to see if you have done your homework. You should never attend an interview unless you know about the company, its direction and the industry in which it plays. <u>If you have done your research, this question gives you an opportunity to show initiative and demonstrate how your experience and qualifications match the company's needs.</u> (3)

The secret to answering this question is being honest about a weakness, but

第七章 | 如何应对面试中的问题（How to Handle the Questions for Interview）

demonstrating how you have turned it into a strength. For example, if you had a problem with organization in the past, demonstrate the steps you took to more effectively keep yourself on track. This will show that you have the ability to recognize aspects of yourself that need improvement, and the initiative to make yourself better. (4)

Sometimes it is hard to come up with a response to this request, particularly if you are coming straight from college and do not have professional experience. Interviewers want to see that you can think critically and develop solutions, regardless of what kind of issue you faced. Even if your problem was not having enough time to study, describe the steps you took to prioritize[4] your schedule. This will demonstrate that you are responsible and can think through situations on your own.

The secret to this question is being specific and selecting an accomplishment that relates to the position. Even if your greatest accomplishment is being on a championship high school basketball team, opt for a more professionally relevant[5] accomplishment. Think of the qualities the company is looking for and develop an example that demonstrates how you can meet the company's needs. (5)

Notes：

[1] vary：变化；呈多样化（+from）　例：That sort of thing varies from person to person.（那种事因人而异。）

[2] succinctly：简洁地；简便地　例：The title should succinctly state the focus of the review.（标题应当简洁陈述该系统评价的核心内容。）

[3] motivate：激励，激发……的积极性　例：Our teachers always motivate students to seek knowledge by ourselves.（我们的老师总是激发学生自己寻求知识。）

[4] prioritize：优先　例：First you have to prioritize your goals, then reach them in order.（首先将你的目标排列优先级，然后再去一一实现。）

[5] relevant：有关的；切题的；恰当的　例：His nationality isn't relevant to whether he is a good lawyer.（他的国籍跟他是不是一个好律师不相关。）

职位实战篇

第八章 申请前厅部工作人员（How to Apply for Jobs in Front Office）

案例导入（Lead-in）

某五星级国际大酒店正面向社会招聘前厅部基层管理人员。通过激烈的角逐，小张和小李都以优秀的表现进入了复试。在复试中，一位主考官向他们提出了同一个问题：你为什么在三年内换了三家酒店？面对相同的问题，他们的答案却截然不同。小张说："我以前待过的三家酒店都不太理想。第一家酒店是国企，整个管理都很混乱，经理们每天都是喝茶聊天，谁有关系谁就升职；第二家酒店是私企，老板为人太小气了，过年发的红包太少，哪留得住人才啊；第三家酒店是外企，管理倒是还不错，可像我这么优秀的人却一直没有被得到重用。"相对小张的高谈阔论，而小李的回答却很简单："是的，我承认自己跳槽确实有些频繁。虽然每份工作都很艰难，但自己却因此学到了很多，也成熟了很多。"听完两人的答案，主考官脸上露出了笑容，似乎对人选已有定数。

问题1 你认为主考官最后选中了哪位求职者？为什么？

问题2 假设你也是求职者，你能用英语回答主考官提出的这个问题吗？

8.1 学习焦点（Focus）

前厅部是负责招徕并接待宾客、销售酒店客房及餐饮娱乐等服务产品、沟通与协调酒店各部门、为客人提供各种综合服务的对客服务部门。

前厅部通常由礼宾部、前台、总机、商务中心、行政楼层及车队等机构组成。本章主要通过对前厅部的工作职能以及前厅部各岗位工作职责来展开进行讨论，使申请前厅部相关岗位的人员了解前厅部的工作职能以及其申请岗位的工作职责，从而能够更好地应对针对具体岗位而来的面试问题。

8.1.1 前厅部工作职能（Functions of Front Office Department）

（1）酒店销售客房

客房销售收入是酒店主要的经济来源，酒店常以客房销售数量及其平均房价来衡量前厅部员工的工作绩效。前厅部除开拓多种渠道接受客房预订业务外，还需负责向未预订而直接抵店的散客推荐客房、确定房价、分配客房、办理入住登记手续等工作。

（2）酒店建立客账

在客人入住期间，前厅部工作人员需为住店客人设立账户并及时更新客户信息，确保账单数据的准确性、及时了解宾客信用情况、有效协助财务部完成每日审核工作，同时还需负责为离店客人办理结账、转账及收款等相关事宜。

（3）酒店控制客房状态

前厅部销售客房的前提条件是准确的客房状态数据。通常客房状态数据来源有两处：一是客房部送来的各层客房状态表，二是前厅部持有的客房状态数据。因此，前厅部员工需将两种房态数据进行仔细核对，看是否有出入。

（4）酒店统计与预测报表

前厅部应随时保持完整的、准确的与经营业务相关的资料，并对各项数据进行记录、统计、分析、预测，分派给其他各部门，然后再由其他各部门呈送上级。

8.1.2 前厅部的各岗位职能（Job Responsibilities in the Front Office Department）

8.1.2.1 酒店前厅部经理的岗位职责（Job Responsibilities of Front Office Manager）

前厅部经理岗位职责如下：

（1）负责制订本部门的经营计划和营业指标；

(2) 做好客源分析，努力掌握旅游市场状况；

(3) 制订部门的工作计划和任务；

(4) 督导和检查部门完成计划的情况；

(5) 控制客房流量与房价；

(6) 检查落实接待重要宾客活动；

(7) 解决客人的严重投诉；

(8) 制订完善的培训计划，保证部门的服务质量；

(9) 完善本部门的各项机构工作及人员合理调配；

(10) 负责本部门与酒店各部门的沟通，做好部门间的协调工作。

8.1.2.2 酒店大堂副理的岗位职责(Job Responsibilities of Duty Manager)

大堂副理的岗位职责如下：

(1) 大堂副理是二十四小时都需值班的岗位，代表酒店处理宾客提出的一切问题。作为大堂副理需熟悉酒店经营情况和各个部门的职责及业务范围、酒店服务项目等情况。

(2) 帮助客人解决疑难。如客人不知道餐厅、娱乐场所、健身地、商品、美容中心等位置，要指给他去的方向或带他去目的地。

(3) 处理投诉。客人投诉的内容有不满，也有建议。受理投诉时不论是什么内容、采取什么方式或出于什么态度，都要以热情、友好和欢迎的态度对待，都要向客人表示道谢。对客人撤诉的内容要作详细记录，并与被投诉的部门主管和个人核实。将核实的情况和处理结果用口头或书面形式答复客人，使客人感到处理是实事求是的、是负责任的，从而提高对酒店的信心。

(4) 注意大堂的秩序和客人的安全。若秩序混乱或有不安全的因素，要进行干预或维持，也可指示保安人员进行维持或干预，保持大堂的肃静和高雅。

(5) "VIP"客人抵离酒店时，大堂副理应陪同总经理、部门经理在门前迎送宾客。

(6) 对于大堂发生的一切事情或处理不了的问题要及时向部门经理或总经理汇报；每隔一段时间，将积累的数据及处理的有关事项整理成文件，通报全体管理层，以便引起各级领导的关注和重视。

8.1.2.3 宾客关系主任的岗位职责(Job Responsibilities of Guest Relation Officer)

宾客关系主任的岗位职责如下：

(1)对酒店内每天的餐饮安排需非常了解；

(2)欢迎和引领贵宾到客房；

(3)负责处理客人的投诉；

(4)留意酒店公众地方的安全和秩序；

(5)负责带客人参观了解酒店的设备；

(6)做好与其他部门的工作协调；

(7)大堂副理不在时代其行使权力。

8.1.2.4 酒店前台接待的岗位职责(Job Responsibilities of Receptionist)

前台接待的岗位职责如下：

(1)受理电话、传真、互联网等不同形式的客房预订,将订房资料录入电脑并传达给相关部门和岗位；

(2)处理销售部或其他部门发来的预订单；

(3)及时按工作标准及程序进行预订变更、取消等数据处理；

(4)检查、核实当日及次日抵达酒店的预订信息,做好预订准备工作；

(5)为客人办理入住登记手续,安排房间；

(6)为客人办理换房、加床续住等手续；

(7)负责保管、制作和发放客房钥匙卡；

(8)按规定填写、录入并统计入住散客及团队登记单；

(9)认真核对上一个班次输入电脑的客人资料,及时准确地输入当班的客人资料；

(10)按规定登记、录入和发送境外客人户籍资料；

(11)认真细致做好交接班工作,保证工作的延续性；

(12)为客人做好结账工作。

8.1.2.5 行李员的岗位职责(Job Responsibilities of Bellman)

行李员的岗位职责如下：

(1)协助住客搬运行李；

(2)代客人交收信件、包裹、便条等；

(3) 对客人保持友善、整洁及称职之形象；

(4) 向客人提供优良及有效率的服务；

(5) 听取住客意见及解答住客的疑难问题；

(6) 尽量满足住客的特别要求,如代客包装其物品等；

(7) 负责所有电话询问及柜台询问事宜；

(8) 代理行李保管事宜和签发行李取索标签事宜。

8.1.2.6 总机的岗位职责(Job Responsibilities of Operator)

总机的岗位职责如下：

(1) 按工作程序迅速、准确地转接每一个电话；

(2) 对客人的询问要热情、有礼、迅速地应答；

(3) 主动帮助宾客查找电话号码或为住客保密电话；

(4) 准确地为客人提供叫醒服务；

(5) 掌握店内组织机构,熟悉店内主要负责人和各部经理的姓名、声音；

(6) 熟悉市内常用电话号码；

(7) 熟悉有关问讯的知识；

(8) 掌握总机房各项设备的功能,操作时懂得充分利用各功能键及注意事项。

8.1.3 面试中常见的专业问题

Interview sample questions of Front office：

(1) What do you know about the roles and responsibilities of front desk staff in a hotel?

(2) What made you choose to apply for Front office?

(3) What have you learned from your past jobs?

(4) What do you know about the position of Front office?

(5) What are key tasks for Front office?

(6) What tertiary qualifications have you attained that related to Front office?

(7) What is the most recent skill you have learned that related to Front office?

(8) What are your strengths and weaknesses?

(9) Please elaborate about the skills and qualifications that you have for this post?

(10) Where would you like to be in five years? Ten years?

8.1.4 常用专业词汇

Vocabulary

Front Desk Manager/Front Office Manager		前台经理	
Front Office Supervisor	前台主管	Lobby Assistant Manager	大堂副理
Duty Manager	值班经理	Receptionist	前台接待
Bellman	行礼员	Operator	总机服务员
GRO (Guest Relation Officer)		顾客关系代表	
Doorman	门童	Arrival expected	预计到达人员
Departure expected	预计离店人员	Due out	即将到期
Overdue	过期	Check-in	入住
Check-out	退房	Executive Floor	行政楼层

8.2 英语情景对话(Dialogues)

8.2.1 Applying for an operator

(Mr. Wong, the Manager of Personal department, is talking to Miss Chen who is applying for the position as an operator. A = Mr. Wong, B = Miss Chen)

A：Ah-Miss Chen? Good to see you. Thank you for coming in to the interview. Now, let me see. You are applying for the vacancy we have for an English telephone operator. Isn't that right?

B：Yes, that's right.

A：And you're the senior student majored in Tourism English in Wuhan Optic Valley College.

B：Yes, I expect to graduate in the summer of 2011.

A：Well, Tourism English, can you tell me something about your major?

B：Actually, I learned a lot of knowledge and skills about hotel management, and

English also plays a very important role in our curriculum[1]. So I'm looking for a career in hospitality industry, with my languages as a useful back-up.

A: Do you have any experience on the switchboard?

B: Yes. Our college arranged the hotel practice for us in the second school year. So I have been a telephone operator in Holiday Inn in Shenzhen for one year, where I have done a good job and practiced English a lot.

A: OK, can you describe the duties of an operator?

B: Of course. As an operator, I must ensure that each guest has a safe and enjoyable stay. Coordinate[2] reservations, maintenance[3]. And decide on marketing initiatives for the hotel and oversee the hotel's profits and computer system.

A: Well, how do you think this job?

B: Frankly speaking, it's not an easy job. During my internship, I sometimes had to work more than 40 hours a week and be on call in case of emergencies. Though it is a little tough, I like it very much. Because it's full of challenges.

A: Can you tell me something about your achievements?

B: Yes, I got the title of excellent hotel attendant in the hotel I practiced in. And I get scholarship every year.

A: What do you know about our hotel?

B: This five-star hotel belongs to the world famous hotel brand which has got a very high reputation[4] and enjoyed the booming business.

A: What do you comment on your character?

B: I think I'm an optimistic[5] person who has an open-minded attitude. I enjoy helping others, which brought me a lot of friends. On the other hand, I don't know how to refuse something or somebody which I don't like sometimes. I have been trying to improve it.

A: OK, very glad to have a talk with you. Is there anything you want to ask about?

B: When will I hear from you?

A: We will call you next Monday.

B: Thank you. I will be looking forward to seeing you again.

Notes:

[1] curriculum:学校的全部课程　例:The student is very knowledgeable because he also studies things not in the curriculum. (这个学生知识很丰富,因为在学校课程以外他还学习别的东西。)

[2] coordinate:协调,调节,使调和　例:If we coordinate our efforts we should be able to win the game. (如果我们同心协力,我们应该能够打赢这场比赛。)

[3] maintenance:维持,保持　例:The maintenance of law and order is of vital importance. (法律与秩序的维持是至关重要的。)

[4] reputation:名誉,名声(+for)　例:The store has an excellent reputation for fair dealing. (该店买卖公平,声誉极佳。)

[5] optimistic:乐观的,乐观主义的　例:He is optimistic about the future. (他对未来很乐观。)

8.2.2 Applying for a job as receptionist

(Alice is attending an interview, and now she is talking with Frank West, the Front Office Manager.)

Alice: Good afternoon, Mr. West, nice to meet you.

Frank: Nice to meet you. Please have a seat.

Alice: Thank you.

Frank: Alice, right?

Alice: Yes, sir.

Frank: Ok, Alice, are you still in wonderland[1]? I'm just kidding. By the way, how do you get the information that there is a receptionist position available in our hotel?

Alice: I've seen it from your homepage, sir.

Frank: I see. According to your resume, you already have one year experience as a receptionist in Ramada Plaza Hotel. It's been quite some time. We both know that being a receptionist is very tough job, the night shift or the complaints from guests sometimes can really stress you out[2], so why do you choose this position to start your career?

第八章 | 申请前厅部工作人员（How to Apply for Jobs in Front Office）

Alice: Well, I really enjoy working with people and helping them. During this one year as a receptionist I have learned some skills in terms of[3] guest service, and I receive three letters of commendation from the guests, which encourage me very much. I really love this job, I sincerely want to build my career in front office department.

Frank: Ok. Can you tell me what the Front Office functions as?

Alice: Well, in my opinion the Front Office Department is not only the "shop window", but also the "nerve center" of the hotel. Check ins/check outs, guest requests, concierge services and promotion of in-house activities are all handled here.

Frank: Yes, you make a point. Can you tell something about your working duties?

Alice: As you know, being a receptionist, welcome and check-in of guests and check-out departing guests using the hotel's accounting system are my primary working duties, and what's more I am seen as a main point of contact for guests, so I have to deal with enquiries[4] and complaints efficiently.

Frank: Hmm, besides performing check in and check out procedure accurately, deal efficiently with enquiries and complaints from our guests are also very important. Because the efficiency of our work really influences[5] a guest's first impressions of the hotel so everything must always be at its very best.

Alice: Mr. West, I'll keep that in mind.

Notes:

[1] wonderland: 奇幻之地、仙境　例: A trip to lapland truly allows you to experience a winter wonderland! （拉普兰之旅真会让你置身冬日仙境！）

[2] stress out: ①迫于压力使得神经紧张　例: I don't want my guests to stress out over what to make when they invite me over for dinner. （我不希望客人们在回请我时过于在意为我做什么。）②强调 As usual we must stress out that all bets are off if we lose the 8200 level on the Dow Jones industrial average（照例我们必须强调，如果道琼斯工业平均指数失守8200点，所有的看涨判断将自动失效。）

[3] in terms of: 根据，按照，用……的话，在……方面　例: Follow client requirements in terms of product development, price, quality and shipment. （根据客户

需求进行产品开发、报价、品质控制以及出货协调。）

〔4〕enquiry：询问　例：Handle telephone enquiries and attend to clients' needs promptly.（及时处理电话询问并尽量满足客户需求。）

〔5〕influence：影响　例：His miserable childhood influences his personality seriously.（他的可怜的童年严重影响了他的个性。）

8.3　学以致用(Transference)

1. Work in pairs. Look at the following pictures and tell your partner who are supposed to be working at hotels.

(1)　　(2)　　(3)　　(4)

(5)　　(6)　　(7)　　(8)

2. 请为下列岗位与其工作职责配对。

(1) Bellhop

(2) Front Desk Supervise

(3) Reservation Agent

(4) Receptionist

(5) Assist of FOM

第八章 | 申请前厅部工作人员 (How to Apply for Jobs in Front Office)

A. Ensure your shift team have an up-to-date knowledge of hotel products, services and pricing along with any special promotional offers. Advise your shift team of any special events or VIP guests in the hotel that day. Monitor the appearance, standards and performance of Team Members with an emphasis on training and team work.

B. Actively converting enquiries into contracted business. Responding positively to sales enquiries to develop future sales leads. Responding to all customers in a highly professional manner, including ensuring all bookings are completed accurately to the customer's needs.

C. Escorts hotel guests to their rooms, carries the luggage, and opens the door. He or she might also offer information about hotel services (room service, laundry, wake-up calls, etc) and tidbits about local attractions.

D. Check the guest arrival reports in advance and liaise daily with Housekeeping on room allocation for VIP guests. Be responsible for special room assignments and suite occupancies. Welcome and check of in VIP guests, escort them to the Executive Lounge and their room. Ensure all VIP room standards are met and amenities are in place before arrival.

E. Welcome and check in of guests, including processing of group arrivals. Check out departing guests using the hotel's accounting system. Be seen as a main point of contact for guests, dealing efficiently with enquiries and any complaints.

3. Look at the questions and answers. Please mark "√" in front of the answer if you think it is proper.

(1) Q: Why should I hire you?

☐ A: Because I am the best candidate. You see, unlike others, I am beautiful, smart, and have a good command of languages. Everybody likes me. So why not choose me?

(2) Q: Why did you choose us?

☐ A: As we all know, your group is one of the best hotel in the word and enjoying a booming business. So I think I can learn a lot in your hotel, especially improving my language skill. Trust me, I am really a good learner.

(3) Q: How did you prepare for this interview?

　　□ A: When I found this position posted on the internet I was immediately interested. I checked out the company website and mission statement, looked at the bios of company founders and executives, and was impressed.

(4) Q: What is your salary expectation for this job?

　　□ A: When I worked for ABC hotel as an intern last year, I earned 2000 RMB each month. So if I were employed by you, you should pay at least more than 2500 RMB each month.

(5) Q: How fast do you think that you will adjust in our hotel?

　　□ A: I believe that life around us changes, sometimes for the good and sometimes for the bad. One must be prepared to accept and deal with every new, challenging situation.

4. Listen to the job vacancy advertisement and fill in the missing information in the spaces.

Hotel Equatorial

The Equatorial Group of Hotels has ___(1)___ itself as a leading operator of hotels in Asia with over ___(2)___ years of experience in the hospitality industry. Our focus is the advancement of the Group's interest and business in all aspects. Individual dedication is essential in meeting this goal.

We are currently looking for an exceptional individual to fill the following vacancy:

___(3)___

Workplace: Kuala Lumpur-Golden Triangle

Responsibilities:

Responsible for handling ___(4)___ requests, maintaining an accurate and updated ___(5)___ system.

Requirements:

At least 1 year working experience in a ___(6)___ capacity.

Proficient in written & spoken English & Bahasa Malaysia.

___(7)___ personality.

第八章 申请前厅部工作人员（How to Apply for Jobs in Front Office）

Computer literate.

Graduates from hotel colleges are also __(8)__ to apply.

Ability to converse in Mandarin/Cantonese would be an added advantage.

If your profile meets our requirements and you would like to join our team, please apply online confidentially.

Address: __(9)__

Only shortlisted candidates will be called for an interview. If your profile meets our requirements and you would like to join our team, please apply online __(10)__ .

5. Complete the following dialogues.

Dialogue A

A: This interview is mostly to test your English, so just relax, and let's chat, shall we?

B: __(1)__ .

A: Do you think you are rather extroverted or __(2)__ ?

B: Well, sometimes I like to be by myself, but most of the time I __(3)__ being with a group of people, so I guess I am rather __(4)__ .

A: One of the most important requirements for the job is the ability to speak English. Do you think you can use English to __(5)__ with the foreign guests?

B: Yes, I think I can. I've been __(6)__ an evening course for English conversation for two years.

A: Why do you want to be __(7)__ ?

B: I've been a receptionist before; I like doing it and am very __(8)__ at it. I can do multi-task and handle interruption well. I am very organized and I like the challenge of trying to stay organized while a lot of different things are going on.

A: All right, then. We'll get in __(9)__ with you within a week. Thank you for coming today.

B: __(10)__ .

(1) All right   (2) introverted   (3) prefer   (4) extroverted   (5) communicate
(6) attending   (7) a receptionist   (8) good   (9) touch   (10) Than you

Dialogue B

A: (1) , Miss Black?

B: I'm 1.65 meters tall.

A: Are you wearing (2) ?

B: NO, my eyesight is very good. A: Have you ever had any serious (3) ?

B: No, I've always been in good health.

A: Your resume says you are working as a receptionist in Hilton Hotel. Why do you want to change the job?

B: Well, I (4) for a new challenge, more responsibility, experience and a change of environment.

A: What is the most important thing do you think for a hotel employee?

B: Try to make the guest feel at home.

A: Tell me what special features a receptionist should have?

B: I think a receptionist should be passionate, courteous and (5) . Only in this way guests will feel welcomed and relax during their stay.

A: All right. You will be (6) us within 5 days. Thank you for your coming.

6. Cloze

How to Answer Hotel Guest Services and Front Desk Interview Questions

Your response really (1) on exactly the type of interview question asked. While interviewing skills as a hiring manager or job applicant can be quite an in depth topic and (2) the scope of this post, we have provided a quick lesson on how you can improve your interview skills. We have chosen to briefly cover the behavioral question because this is where we see most people (3) .

To ensure that you provide good answers consistently we advise that you follow a structured (4) when responding to behavioral type questions. Two effective techniques to use are "STAR" (situation, task, action, result) and "PAR" (problem, action, result). These techniques are very similar to one another, so for illustrative purposes, we will discuss the STAR method.

To use the STAR technique, simply describe each element in your interview answer.

第八章 申请前厅部工作人员(How to Apply for Jobs in Front Office)

So with the star technique, begin by __(5)__ the situation. Here you want to quickly give context to the interviewer (where, when, etc). Next clearly describe your task, that is what were you tasked to do in this situation. Now it is time to describe the steps or action you took to __(6)__ your task. Lastly, describe the results that you achieved. Sounds simple right? Well it is simple, but the secret is to practice __(7)__ following this structure. By following structure, you will ensure that you provide complete answers and do not __(8)__ vital pieces of information. For more information see our articles and courses on interviewing skills.

(1) A. targeted   B. focus   C. depends   D. rely
(2) A. within   B. beyond   C. over   D. in
(3) A. hesitate   B. scary   C. struggle   D. fight for
(4) A. instruction B. approach   C. way   D. channel
(5) A. describing B. explaining C. demonstrating D. telling
(6) A. finish   B. complete   C. match   D. motivate
(7) A. answering   B. responding C. assessing   D. linking
(8) A. omit   B. mention   C. involve   D. skip

8.4 补充英语阅读(Reading)

1. 阅读下列课文并为其找出最合适的标题。

   A. Front Office Department Function in Hotel

   B. Introduction of Front Office

   C. What Is the Importance of Front Office Department

   D. What is the Front Office Department in Hotel Operations

2. 根据课文内容判断正(T)误(F)。

   (1) The Front Office function of a Hotel is to act as back office of the hotel, primarily by greeting hotel patrons and checking in guests. (   )

   (2) Members of the front-office staff welcome the guests, carry their luggage, help them register, give them their room keys and mail, answer questions about the

activities in the hotel and surrounding area, and finally check them out. (　　)

(3) Receptionists is only responsible for check in and check out, not including the task of organizing databases. (　　)

(4) In some hotels, the reservation department can, on real time, access the number and types of rooms available, various room rates, and furnishings, along with the various facilities existing in the hotel. (　　)

(5) The Front Office also provides assistance to guests during their stay, completes their accommodation, food and beverage accounts and receives payment from guests. (　　)

What Is the Importance of Front Office Department?

The front office department is extremely important because in most cases the front desk is the first thing that a visitor will see. In a sense, the front office department is an introduction to the hotel. How successfully the front office department runs is a reflection of the organization skills of the hotel as a whole. A well-presented[1], well organized front office department will give a great first impression to visitors. A frantic[2], unorganized[3] front desk will immediately give visitors a sense of unease[4] and a negative impression about the company.

Front office departments are important to a hotel as they provide a number of benefits. A front office department can act as a welcome point to greet guests and customers, introducing them to the hotel and some of the service items before they actually check-in.

A front office department that will be used as an area for visitors to wait. An area with chairs, an option to get drinks and things to look at make a much nicer environment for guests to wait in rather than wandering around the hotel lobby.

A well-run front desk that ensures good communication between the hotel and its guest reflects the approach of the hotel as a whole. The department is also important when there is a need for multi-tasking. Receptionists can have daily tasks that vary from organizing databases to arranging meetings to filing paperwork.

Notes:

[1] well-presented:优质的、体面的　例:If the candidate delivers a well-presented, timely, and effective solution during the interview, our company is likely to hire that person. (如果面试者能在面试过程中呈现一个优质有效的解决方案,我们公司很可能会雇用他。)

[2] frantic:(因喜悦,愤怒等)发狂似的(+with)　例:The mother was frantic with grief at the loss of her child. (母亲因失去孩子悲恸欲绝。)

[3] unorganized:没有条理的,无组织的　例:You're like me, a bit unorganized, I put my documents everywhere. (你和我一样,有一点没有条理,我到处放我的文件。)

[4] unease:心神不安、不舒服　例:Maurice still felt the unease of wrongdoing. (莫里斯仍然怀有做了坏事的不安感。)

第九章 申请餐饮部工作人员
(How to Apply for Jobs in Food and Beverage Department)

案例导入(Lead-in)

某酒店总经理王某从国内某知名旅游院校招聘了高才生小张担任其助理,由于这个年轻小伙子亲和力强、反应敏捷且英语流利,助理工作做得十分出色,深得王总喜爱。两年后,正值原餐饮部经理跳槽,王总认为应该给小张一个发展的机会,于是就把他任命为酒店餐饮部经理。谁知在半年内,先后有三个下属离职,部门工作陷入混乱,其他部门对餐饮部也抱怨颇多。原来小张从学校直接到酒店担任高管助理,并不熟悉餐饮部服务流程和业务,也不具备管理工作的经验,这就导致其决策往往理想化,缺乏专业性,且与同级和下属的沟通方式也不到位,常常让下属深感委屈。同时,小张还认为工作只需向总经理汇报,没有必要考虑其他部门的利益。因而,其开展的工作也得不到他人的支持。最终,在各种内部压力下,小张也引咎递交了辞职信。

问题1　你认为是哪些原因导致小张最终递交了辞职信?

问题2　你认为酒店餐饮部经理应该具备哪些能力和素质?

9.1 学习焦点(Focus)

酒店餐饮部是酒店一个极其重要的部门,是酒店经济收入的主要来源之一。

酒店餐饮部的岗位主要有餐饮总监、餐饮总监助理、行政总厨、餐饮部文员、中

第九章 申请餐饮部工作人员(How to Apply for Jobs in Food and Beverage Department)

餐厅经理、中餐厅领班、中餐厅迎宾员、中餐厅服务员、中餐厅传菜员、中餐厅划菜员、中餐厅酒水员、西餐厅经理、西餐厅领班、西餐厅迎领员、西餐厅服务员、宴会厅经理、宴会厅领班、餐务预订员、宴会服务员、大堂吧领班、大堂吧服务员、大堂吧调酒员、中餐厨师长、中餐热菜领班、炉台厨师、打荷厨师、中式点心厨师、中餐冷菜厨师、管事组领班等岗位。通常餐饮部是整个酒店员工人数最多的一个部门。本章主要通过对餐饮部的工作职能以及餐饮部各岗位工作职责来展开进行讨论,使申请餐饮部相关岗位的人员了解餐饮部的工作职能以及其申请岗位的工作职责,从而能够更好地应对针对具体岗位而来的面试问题。

9.1.1 餐饮部的工作职能(Functions of Food & Beverage Department)

(1)掌握市场需求、合理制定菜单。餐饮部应了解本酒店目标客源市场的消费特点,掌握不同年龄、不同性别、不同职业、不同国籍和民族、不同宗教信仰的客人的饮食习惯,并在此基础上制定出能够迎合目标客源市场的菜单,满足客人对餐饮服务的各种需求。

(2)进行餐饮创新、创造经营特色。酒店餐饮服务应具有吸引客人并与其他酒店和社会餐馆、酒楼竞争的能力,最重要的是必须创造自己的经营特色。这就要求餐饮部应努力挖掘人员潜力,积极继承传统,研究开发新的菜点品种,并配以与之相适应的餐饮环境及特色服务。

(3)加强餐饮推销、增加营业收入。餐饮部应在酒店营销计划的指导下,研究、分析餐饮客人的消费需求,精心选择推销计划,开展各种形式的促销活动,积极招徕各种宴会,努力做好节假日和酒店特色餐饮的宣传推销,以争取更多的客源并尽力提高客人的平均消费水平。

(4)控制餐饮成本,提高盈利水平。餐饮经营的目的是在满足客人饮食需求的基础上为酒店创造利润,因此,餐饮部应加强培训,提高服务员的工作效率,从而降低人力成本,同时减少低值易耗品的消耗,餐饮部应确定低值易耗品的消耗标准,增加盈利。

9.1.2 餐饮部各岗位职责(Job Responsibilities in the Food & Beverage Department)

9.1.2.1 餐饮部经理岗位职责(Job Responsibilities of Food & Beverage Manager)

餐饮部经理岗位职责如下：

(1)负责酒店餐饮部的全面工作；

(2)认真执行总经理下达的各项工作任务和工作指标,对餐饮部的经营情况负有重要的责任；

(3)制订餐饮部的营业政策和经营计划；

(4)拟订餐饮部每年的预算方案和营业指标、审阅餐饮部各单位每天的营业报表、进行营业分析并作出相应的经营决策；

(5)主持日常餐饮部的部门会议,协调部门内部各单位的工作,使其协调一致地顺利进行；

(6)审阅和批示部属各单位和个人呈交的报告及各项申请；

(7)与行政总厨、大厨、宴会部研究如何提高食品的质量,创制新的菜色品种；制定或修订年、季、月、周、日的餐牌,制定食品及饮料的成本标准；

(8)参加总经理召开的各部经理例会及业务协调会议,与各界建立良好的公共关系；

(9)对部属管理人员的工作进行督导,帮助他们不断提高业务能力水平；

(10)负责督促部属员工的服务情况,使餐饮部的服务档次得以提高。

9.1.2.2 餐饮部领班岗位职责(Job Responsibilities of Restaurant Captain)

餐饮部领班岗位职责如下：

(1)在部门经理的领导下,检查落实部门规章制度的执行情况和各项工作的完成情况；

(2)检查当班服务员的工作着装及个人仪表；

(3)安排、带领、督促、检查员工使其做好营业前的各项准备工作并及时、准确地向经理反映部门情况、汇报各员工的工作表现；

(4)做好各项班次物品、单据交接工作；

(5)熟悉业务,在工作中起模范带头作用,协助经理增强本部门员工的凝聚力；

第九章 │ 申请餐饮部工作人员（How to Apply for Jobs in Food and Beverage Department）

(6) 加强现场管理意识，及时处理突发事件，带领员工不断提高服务质量；

(7) 加强公关意识，树立宾馆酒店良好的形象；

(8) 做好员工的考勤排休工作；

(9) 主持每周班务会，听取服务员的工作汇报，及时总结并发挥主观能动性，对经营管理上的不足之处提出自己的意见、设想，并上报经理；

(10) 完成上级领导交办的其他工作。

9.1.2.3 餐厅服务员岗位职责（Job Responsibilities of Waiter）

餐饮部服务员岗位职责如下：

(1) 熟悉本餐厅的工作流程；

(2) 做好上班前后的餐厅准备工作，积极检查备用餐具是否齐全，餐台上器皿是否整洁齐全；

(3) 工作时要做到口勤、眼勤、手勤和脚勤，并及时了解客人心态、需求，为顾客提供服务；

(4) 要有牢固的业务操作知识，掌握及懂得客人需要的每份饮料及食物的用餐规律；

(5) 接待顾客应主动、热情、礼貌、耐心、周到，使顾客有宾至如归之感；

(6) 迎宾员带客到位，服务员应主动上前替客人拉椅子，做好接待工作；

(7) 运用礼貌语言，为客人提供最佳服务，做到文明有礼、掌握原则、有问必答、言简意赅；

(8) 善于向顾客介绍和推销本餐厅饮品及特色菜点；

(9) 有较强的工作责任心，有独立处理事务的能力，发现问题及时上报，班前或班后提出问题并及时转告客人提出的意见；

(10) 配合领班工作，服从领班或以上领导指挥，团结及帮助同事工作；

(11) 加强业务知识的学习，不断掌握服务技能，提高服务质量。

9.1.2.4 调酒员岗位职责（Job Responsibilities of Bartender）

调酒员岗位职责如下：

(1) 按照酒店标准和客人要求，负责吧台酒水饮品的供应工作，按程序补充酒水；

(2) 负责饮品的领取、保管和销售工作，每日进行一次清点并负责本吧台售出

酒水的保存;

（3）负责为客人调制鸡尾酒，管理酒吧的玻璃杯、器皿和设备;

（4）负责填报《酒水销售盘点日报表》，做到报表和实物相符，销售量和账目相符;

（5）负责工作区域的卫生，包括设备、用具的卫生，必要时协助服务员进行打扫;

（6）积极参加各种技术培训，不断提高业务水平。

9.1.2.5 迎宾员岗位职责（Job Responsibilities of Restaurant Hostess）

迎宾员岗位职责如下：

（1）熟悉餐厅的工作流程;

（2）仪容仪表端庄大方，衣着整洁，精神饱满;

（3）服从领班的领导指挥，积极配合餐厅服务员的接待工作;

（4）运用礼貌语言和客人说话;

（5）掌握及了解客人的需求，迎接客人到其满意的座位上，并主动递上菜单、饮品单，待服务员迎上前再离去;

（6）迎送客人要面带笑容，主动、热情、礼貌，做到客到有请声、客问有应声、客走有送声;

（7）走路要注意礼让，客过要让路，同行不抢道，迎客走在前，送客走在后;

（8）不断加强业务知识学习，提高服务水准和工作质量。

9.1.3 面试中常见的专业问题

Interview questions samples of Food & Beverage Department:

（1）Can you describe your working routine?

（2）If a regular customer is always complaining about a certain kind of dish, how do you deal with this kind of situation?

（3）What should you pay attention to when you are taking orders for guests?

（4）What should you pay attention to when you are doing reservation for guests?

（5）Can you tell me your approach to up-selling Food and Beverage products?

（6）How much do you know about our hotel?

(7) How do you react to the critics your boss gives to you?

(8) What kinds of qualities and abilities need to be possessed if you want to be successful in the hospitality industry?

(9) Could you tell me your approach to ensure each meal and beverage given to customers is of highest quality?

(10) What was your worst experience with a customer at your last serving job?

9.1.4 常用专业词汇

Vocabulary

Food & Beverage Department	餐饮部	hostess	咨客
waiter/waitress	服务员	bartender	调酒员
Buffet	自助餐厅	A la carte	零点餐厅
Lobby Lounge	大堂吧	Gourmet Shop	美食店
Western restaurant	西餐厅	Chinese restaurant	中餐厅
appetizer/starter	开胃菜	main course	主菜
desert	甜点	snack	零食
French fries	薯条	steak	牛排
well done	全熟	medium	五成熟
rare	三成熟	draft beer	生啤酒
brandy	白兰地	whisky	威士忌
vodka	伏特加		

9.2 英语情景对话(Dialogues)

9.2.1 Applying for an waitress

(Mr. Brown, the Manager of Personal department, is talking to Miss Liu who is applying for the position as an waitress. A = Mr. Brown, B = Miss Liu)

A: Come in, Miss Liu. I am John Brown, the Manager of Personal. What can I do for you?

B: How do you do, Mr. Brown? I am coming for a job interview at ten o'clock this morning.

A: Oh, I see. Take a seat please.

B: Thank you.

A: How can you describe yourself?

B: I'm hard working, reliable[1] and flexible[2]. I have a bubbly[3] personality and love learning new things.

A: What previous jobs have you held?

B: I was a waitress for McDonald's.

A: Did you enjoy your job?

B: Always, of course. I enjoyed serving guests and help them best of all. I was happy when they were happy.

A: How would you describe your last boss?

B: My last boss was terrific. We had clear lines of communication and each of us knew what to expect from the other. There was a high level of trust between us.

A: So why did you leave your last serving job?

B: I'm looking for a bigger challenge and to grow my career. I recently received my degree and want to utilize[4] my educational background in my next position.

A: Do you think you are a good staff?

B: I certainly do think I am a good staff. As you can see from my resume, I have often been the best employee of the month.

A: Why did you choose us?

B: As the old saying goes, "well begun is half done". Your hotel is a famous one in the hospitality industry and boasts a high reputation. I hope to choose your hotel to develop my career. On the other hand, my serving experience and ability to communicate and build customer relationships, which along with my flexibility and language skills, make me a perfect match for this position.

第九章 | 申请餐饮部工作人员(How to Apply for Jobs in Food and Beverage Department)

A: What was your worst experience with a customer at your last serving job?

B: My worst experience is when a customer yelled at me, I tried to stay calm and not to get my emotions involved. I say sorry for the inconvenience and pacify[5] the situation.

A: Great. Do you have any questions for us?

B: How long would our contract be for?

A: We ask our employees to sign two-year contract.

B: Thank you, sir. I do hope the chance to join you in the future.

A: And thank you for your time.

Notes:

[1] reliable:可信赖的;可靠的;确实的　例:I found this to be a reliable brand of washing machines. (我觉得这是一种牌子可靠的洗衣机。)

[2] flexible:变通的;灵活的;易适应的　例:We need a foreign policy that is more flexible. (我们需要更有弹性的外交政策。)

[3] bubbly:有活力的　例:I like her bubbly personality which makes her very easy to be around. (我喜欢她的性格,有活力,很好相处。)

[4] utilize:利用　例:Scientists are trying to find more efficient ways of utilizing solar energy. (科学家正在寻找能更有效地利用太阳能的方法。)

[5] pacify:安抚　例:He tried to pacify his creditors by repaying part of the money. (他为安抚债权人偿还了部分借款。)

9.2.2 Applying for an job as a F&B director

(Michael is attending an interview.)

Michael: Glad to meet you, Ms. Lin.

Lin: Nice to meet you, Michael.

Lin: I am informed that currently you are working for Elysee Hotel as a F&B director, and so far as I know you are actually doing a pretty good job there. I am wondering what triggers[1] you to choose our hotel to build your future career?

Michael: Because I believe a job with Golden Palace Hotel Group which enjoy a high reputation worldwide is never just a job—it's an open door to success, I am really want to be part of this inspiring and stimulating culture that embraces new thinking.

Lin: Good! As you know, being F&B director, especially in this hotel, you have thousands of things to worry, ranging from all food and beverage outlets and services in a hotel to motive employees, but the quality of the food and beverage should always come to first. Could you tell me your approach to ensure each meal and beverage given to customers is of highest quality?

Michael: Yes, Ms. Lin. Ensuring each meal and beverage of highest quality is the most important precondition[2] that we can win over our customers. In order to do that, first of all, I must ensure that diners are served properly and in a timely manner, investigate and resolve customers' complaints about food quality and service, I also put a lot efforts in monitoring orders in the kitchen and working with the chef to remedy[3] any delays in service.

Lin: Hmm, we do need someone who cares about ensuring our customers have a great experience, so that they will remember and will make them want to return. And Michael, you've already been the F&B director for four years, I really want to know how do you motivate[4] your staff?

Michael: There are a lot of ways we can manage to motivate my staff. For example, I always praise the waiters who have "up sold" the most, chefs who added a delectable[5] twist to a menu item, or holding one-on-one meetings with my staff to discover the ways they'd like you to reward them for excellent performance, and hosting regular dinners or outside events where my staff can interact and get to know each other better.

Lin: You really have a way of motivating your staff. Ok, if we decide to hire you, we'll notify you by telephone. Thanks for coming.

Michael: Thank you very much for giving me your time. I'll be expecting your call. Good-bye.

第九章 | 申请餐饮部工作人员(How to Apply for Jobs in Food and Beverage Department)

Notes:

[1] trigger:能引起反应的刺激物[(+for)]　例:Some people say that violent movies are potential triggers for juvenile delinquency.（一些人说暴力影片可能引起青少年犯罪。）

[2] precondition:先决条件、前提条件　例:Raising is a basic precondition for running a successsful election campaign.（募款能力是一个成功竞选的基本先决条件。）

[3] remedy:治疗　例:There is no sure remedy for aids.（艾滋病没有切实有效的治疗方法。）

[4] motivate:激励　例:Our teachers always motivate students to seek knowledge by ourselves.（我们的老师总是激发学生自己寻求知识。）

[5] delectable:美味的　例:You may want to pause to appreciate some people who contributed to the invention of this delectable dessert.（你或许想停下来感谢一下那些对这一美味甜点的问世有所贡献的人。）

9.3　学以致用(Transference)

1. Work in pairs. Read the following hands-wanted adopted from a local evening newspaper and tell what job is on it. Discuss with your partner which job is preferable.

A	B
Responsible for serving alcoholic beverages to passengers in lounges and on decks-minimum of two years beverage-related experience or an equivalent combination of experience and education required.	Responsible for serving passengers, explain the dishes, make recommendations, supervise assistant waiters assigned to their tables-lots of experience and fluent English Language skills required.

C	D
Responsible for a certain serving station in the dining room, supervises all waiters-lots of restaurant and prior cruise ship experience in related position required. Fluent English Language skills required.	Taking care of seating arrangements, service, and overseeing the wait staff for the dining room. Under the maître d' hotel(餐厅领班) are the head waiters, and each of them is responsible for several waiters and busboys. Fluent English Language skills required.

2. After complete the question above, please tell your partner why you think that job is suitable for you? Which words do you think can best describe the job you like?

   interesting   challenging   boring   initiating   pressing   well-paid

   funny   exhausting   time-consuming   troublesome   promising

   amazing   stressful

3. What qualities you think you are equipped with now?

   loyal   firm-willed   initiative   dynamic   ambitious

   absent-minded   timid   open-hearted   diligent   industrious

   conservative   optimistic   sentimental   pessimistic   efficient

4. Look at the questions and answers. Please mark "√" in front of the answer if you think it is proper.

   (1) Q: We require you to come in an hour before busy time, and stay an hour after we close to clean, is that okay? See Answers?

   ☐ A: Yes, I'd loved challenges, the more busy I was the more active and alert I am while working, it makes me even more productive.

   (2) Q: Why did you choose us?

   ☐ A: If I get tipped like that, it is self-evaluation time. First I curse angrily, then I whip the money at the wall.

第九章 | 申请餐饮部工作人员(How to Apply for Jobs in Food and Beverage Department)

(3) Q: If customer were sending something back their ordering to the kitchen complaining about the food, what should you do?

☐ A: I will apologize first, tell them you will correct it to their liking, and then also tell a manager, so they can make sure everything is fine and make any compensations needed.

(4) Q: If customers ask you to pick a meal, what will you suggest?

☐ A: I will strongly let themselves pick their meal, because if I pick the meal for them, and they don't like it, they will blame me for that.

(5) Q: How well can you up selling?

☐ A: You know I am a hardworking man, but I'm really not good at up selling.

5. A hotel manager is explaining the restaurant jobs of the Food & Beverage Department. Fill in the blanks with the proper form of the words given in the brackets.

The food and beverage division is __(1)__ (responsibility) for all of the dining rooms, restaurant-bars, bars, the galleys (kitchens), and provisions. The Food and Beverage Director __(2)__ (run) this department. The dining room manager, or maitred', takes care of __(3)__ (seat) arrangements, service, and __(4)__ (oversee) the wait staff for the main restaurant (dining room). Under the maitre d'are the head waiters, and each of them is responsible for several waiters and busboys. Even though waiters and busboys are __(5)__ (consider) entry level positions, many cruise ships __(6)__ (prefer) those with previous experience from a restaurant or hotel dining room on their resume/CV. Bartenders, wine stewards and cocktail waitresses/waiters must usually __(7)__ (have) prior experience.

6. Listen to the job vacancy advertisement and fill in the missing information in the spaces.

The Berjaya Hotels & Resorts is a group, which name and branding has __(1)__ international reputation in the tourism industry. In line with our aggressive expansion and commitment to excellence, we are urgently __(2)__ high caliber and dynamic individuals to join our operation team.

JAPANESE TEA HOUSE OFFICER

(Pahang - Bukit Tinggi)

Responsibilities:

Assisting Japanese Tea House Manager on the __(3)__ operation of the Japanese Village

Requirements:

Fresh School leaver are welcome to apply as training will be __(4)__.

Preferred Female age between __(5)__ years old

Ability to converse in Mandarin would be an added __(6)__

2 __(7)__ positions available

Applicants should be Malaysian citizens

Benefit:

Meal, __(8)__, transportation to & fro work place provided

Please apply online.

7. Cloze

Once You Have the Job as a Waiter or Waitress

Know that restaurant hours can be very sporadic and unpredictable. A restaurant being busy relies on many factors: the weather, time of day, day of the week, or even on traffic. Some of these factors are impossible to __(1)__. As a result, managers might __(2)__ way too many or way too few servers for each shift and you might have to work much longer or much shorter than expected. Example: you could be scheduled to come in at 11 A.M. and find yourself leaving at 1:15P.M., or you could be scheduled at 10 A.M. and not get out of the door until 4 P.M. Be patient and don't obsess over it because it is not going to make the time go any faster.

Do not take a manager—or anyone in the restaurant industry's—behavior too __(3)__. It is a very __(4)__, busy environment to work in and often these employees are just __(5)__ and overworked. A manager is expected to __(6)__ employees, the schedule, the kitchen, and most importantly, the guests. So if they snap at you and seem like they don't care about your feelings, it's probably just because they don't have

第九章 申请餐饮部工作人员(How to Apply for Jobs in Food and Beverage Department)

time.

Be prepared to make tons of money on some shifts, and barely anything on others. Once again, how busy you are depends on many factors. Instead of getting too __(7)__, realize that the big nights __(8)__ for the crappy ones. So if you make $300 in four hours on a Saturday night, don't be too upset when you make $40 the next morning.

(1) A. explain   B. predict   C. find out   D. know
(2) A. make up   B. calculate   C. schedule   D. check
(3) A. seriously   B. personally   C. sincerely   D. dramatically
(4) A. high-pressured   B. elegant   C. open-ended   D. high end
(5) A. miserable   B. stressed   C. comfortable   D. pathetic
(6) A. look upon   B. manager   C. oversee   D. supervise
(7) A. overwhelmed   B. frustrated   C. emotional   D. excited
(8) A. use up   B. save up   C. make up   D. add up to

9.4 补充英语阅读(Reading)

1. 阅读短文并将下列选项填入文中空白处。

   A. learn the basics before your interview

   B. also study up on the restaurant

   C. show your conversational ability and outgoingness

2. 根据课文内容判断正(T)误(F)。

   (1) According to the passage, most managers won't evaluate their potential staff based on their first impression, because it's not objective. (   )

   (2) You can't add any fashion element in what you are wearing when you attend an interview. (   )

   (3) Managers will link your performance during an interview to how you would approach a table while serving. (   )

(4) Show your conversational ability and outgoingness can increase your chance of being hired. (   )

(5) Study up on the restaurant beforehand is not very necessary. (   )

Preparing for an Interview as a Waiter or Waitress

Just like in any job, your interview is where you can either seal the deal at a restaurant or watch the job slip through your fingers. Most managers know a good serving candidate when they see one, and it's not surprising that the restaurant industry is based largely on first impressions—customers judge a restaurant by the outside, servers often judge guests by their appearances, groups looking to socialize judge by the bar and managers, on a day of the interview, judge applicants by their first impression. They do this for a reason: they know if they get a good impression of you, guests probably will, too.

With that in mind, here are some suggestions for making the best impression possible at an interview.

Firstly, be well-dressed: look clean and professional but also attractive. Ladies, wear something appropriate but don't be afraid to show off fashion sense—restaurant employers appreciate this kind of creativity. Guys—you can't go wrong with a classic suit, but you can also show off some fashion knack—a nice sweater or collared shirt can be just as acceptable.

Secondly, like in any interview, always show up 10 – 15 minutes early, with your resume in hand, looking professional. If you ran around a subway or walked a long time, touch up in the bathroom before you sit down. Managers will look for signs of how you would approach a table while serving, so be as well-put-together as possible.

Thirdly, during the interview, __(1)__. Managers will want to feel secure that you are comfortable with people and have a knack for flowing conversation. However, make sure to not be too casual[1] and always sit up straight, use proper language, and answer questions with confidence (but also diplomatically[2]).

Fourthly, __(2)__. Some restaurants, particularly the high-end[3] ones, might quiz you on your wine or food knowledge. Many managers are known to ask you what certain wines taste like, name different dishes, or identify herbs[4]. It's okay if you don't know every answer—just be confident, because in many cases the manager wants to see your reaction under pressure.

Lastly, ___(3)___. You will be asked if you have any questions, and it is best to have them. It will show that you are interested and have done your own research.

Notes:

[1] casual: 漫不经心的、非正式的　例: Casual attitude will lead to casualties. (漫不经心的态度会造成人员伤亡。)

[2] diplomatically: 圆滑的、婉转的　例: Need more time to resolve situation diplomatically. (要更多的时间圆滑地解决状况。)

[3] high-end: 高端的　例: The company has successfully pushed into the high-end server market. (本公司已成功进入高端服务器市场。)

[4] herb: 草本植物、药草　例: Many herbs are used in traditional Chinese medicine. (很多草本植物都被使用于传统的中药中。)

第十章　申请客房部工作人员（How to Apply for Jobs in Housekeeping Department）

案例导入（Lead-in）

近年来，在全球金融危机的冲击下，我国就业形势不容乐观，尤其是缺乏经验的大学生们，其就业形势更是严峻。据相关媒体报道，从2011年召开的几场高校毕业生就业招聘会上看，今年毕业生的就业观念、就业期望值同往年相比都发生了根本的转变，"先就业后择业，愿意从基层做起"成了许多大学生的共识。几家酒店的招聘人员都向记者表示："和往年相比，今年大学生来应聘的增多，往年大多是中专生，今年应聘的大学生也不乏愿意从事基础性工作如客房服务员，虽然开始工资可能不高，但是如果你真想在酒店干下去，从基层做起反而升迁的机会要更多，而且待遇的逐步提高也需要经历相应的过程。"一名刚应聘酒店客房服务员的大学生对记者说："我觉得客房服务员比起其他部门人员最大的好处就是站得高望得远，尤其能关注到服务细节。虽然现在很辛苦，但我会每天给自己小小的挑战，并且放宽自己的心态，希望可以从中学到更多。"

问题1　你认为一名酒店管理专业的毕业生在找工作时应具备何种心态？
问题2　你认为客房部工作人员应具备怎样的素质呢？

10.1　学习焦点（Focus）

客房服务是酒店必不可少的一项工作，没有一个酒店可以缺少客房部。客房部工作日程的复杂性和不可预料性使得客房部领导与员工之间的沟通极其重要。

第十章 申请客房部工作人员(How to Apply for Jobs in Housekeeping Department)

本章主要通过对客房部的工作职能以及客房部各岗位工作职责来展开进行讨论,使申请客房部相关岗位的人员了解客房部的工作职能以及其申请岗位的工作职责,从而能够更好地应对针对具体岗位而来的面试问题。

10.1.1 客房部的工作职能(Functions of Housekeeping Department)

客房部是酒店的主要创收部门。客房部的经营管理和服务水准,直接影响着酒店的形象、声誉和经营效益。

客房部的主要职能是:认真执行总经理的工作指令,切实贯彻"以市场为导向,以成本为中心,以质量为生命"的经营管理方针和"让客人完全满意"的服务宗旨,坚持服务现场管理,实行规范服务,强化质量管理,保证优质高效的对客服务;广泛搜集住店客人的信息,沟通与协调酒店和客人之间的关系,赢得良好的形象和声誉;贯彻落实酒店制定的经营目标,加强预算管理和成本核算,严格控制成本费用,保证预算目标的实现。

10.1.2 客房部的各岗位职责(Job Responsibilities in the Housekeeping Department)

10.1.2.1 客房部经理的岗位职责(Job Responsibilities of Housekeeping Manager)

客房部经理的岗位职责如下:

(1)贯彻执行酒店副总经理的经营管理指令;

(2)根据酒店的经营方针和目标,负责编制客房部预算方案,制订各项业务计划,并有效实施与监控,实现预期目标;

(3)以市场为导向,研究并掌握市场的变化和发展情况,适时调整经营策略,努力创收,严格控制成本,降低消耗,以最小的成本获取最大的经济效益;

(4)主持部门工作例会,听取汇报,督促工作进度,解决工作中的问题;

(5)负责客房部的安全管理工作,遵照"谁主管,谁负责"的安全责任制,督促本部门各管区落实各项安全管理制度,切实做好安全防范工作;

(6)负责客房部的日常质量管理,检查督促各管区并严格按照工作规范和质量要求进行工作,实行规范作业,每日巡视本部门各管区一次以上,抽查各类客房10间以上;

(7)加强本部门与酒店其他部门的联系,使各部门工作得到有效开展;

(8)建立良好的客户关系,广泛听取和搜集客人意见,处理投诉,不断改进工作;

(9)审阅各管区每天的业务报表,密切注意客情,掌握重要接待任务情况;

(10)负责客房设施设备的使用管理工作,督促各管区做好日常的维护保养和清洁工作,定期进行考核检查;参与客房的改造和更新装修工作;

(11)考核各管区经理、主管的工作业绩,激励员工的积极性,不断提高管理效能。

10.1.2.2 公共区域(PA)主管的工作职责(Job Responsibilities of Public Area Supervisor)

公共区域(PA)主管的工作职责如下:

(1)执行客房部经理指令,并向其报告工作;

(2)组织员工严格按照工作规范和质量标准做好酒店公共区域的清洁和绿化工作;

(3)加强费用开支控制,负责管区内财产和物料用品的管理和领用,做好维护保养和保管工作,发现设备故障及时报修或提出更新意见;

(4)负责对班组工作的考核,员工考勤和业务培训;

(5)做好与各部门的沟通联系,协调工作。

10.1.2.3 客房楼层主管的工作职责(Job Responsibilities of Floor Supervisor)

客房楼层主管的工作职责如下:

(1)执行客房部经理的工作指令,向其报告工作;

(2)了解当天住客情况及房态,监督楼层与前台的联系和协调工作,确保房间正常及时地销售;

(3)认真做好员工的服务宗旨教育和岗位业务培训,保证优质规范服务;

(4)每天巡视楼层,检查管区内30%住客房和OK房,督导领班、服务员的工作情况;

(5)组织、控制每周的卫生清洁计划;

(6)负责处理客人的遗留物品、特殊要求及投诉;

(7)主持领班每天的例会和组织员工全会,并做好记录;

(8)负责管区的成本费用控制,督导和检查库房保管员使其做好财产物料的管理工作;

第十章 申请客房部工作人员（How to Apply for Jobs in Housekeeping Department）

（9）教育和督导员工做好维护保养和报修工作，定期安排设备维修、用品添置和更新改造计划；

（10）坚持现场督导和管理，保证客房服务中心24小时电话接听及监控台的服务质量，发现问题时及时进行指导和纠正；

（11）做好与其他部门的沟通协调工作。

10.1.2.4 楼层领班的工作职责（Job Responsibilities of Floor Captain）

楼层领班的工作职责如下：

（1）执行上级领导的工作指令并报告工作；

（2）负责自己管区内的日常工作安排；

（3）负责检查本班组员工的仪容仪表及工作表现；

（4）负责检查本楼面客房、公共区域卫生及安全情况；

（5）坚持让客人完全满意的服务宗旨，督导和带领员工按客房服务规范和质量标准做好服务工作；

（6）做好对新员工的带教工作，使之尽快适应工作要求；

（7）负责本楼层的设施设备的维修保养和财产的保管；

（8）加强成本费用控制，做好物料用品的管理领用和发放；

（9）负责本楼层房间酒水的消费统计、领取、发放与配置；

（10）做好交接记录。

10.1.2.5 客房清洁员的工作职责（Job Responsibilities of Housekeeper）

客房清洁员的工作职责如下：

（1）服从领班的工作安排；

（2）按照客房清洁流程和质量标准，做好客房和责任区内日常清洁工作；

（3）保持楼层责任区域内环境通道和工作间的干净整洁；

（4）负责预退客房的检查和报账工作；

（5）协助领班做好VIP房和有特殊要求房的布置；

（6）协助洗衣房做好客衣的分送工作；

（7）按照规格要求布置客房，检查房内各类家具和设备的完好情况，及时报告和报修；

（8）负责及时上报，处理突发事件；

（9）做好当班工作记录和交接班工作。

10.1.3 面试中常见的专业问题

Interview questions samples of Housekeeping Department：

（1）Can you tell me the responsibilities of being a housekeeper in your perspective?

（2）What's the maximum time you take for cleaning an occupied room and how much for departure room?

（3）What are the most important skills required to become a good housekeeper?

（4）What do you know about the position of housekeeper?

（5）What previous experience do you have within a housekeeping role?

（6）How would you handle an irate guest?

（7）What was your response when the guest complained his room status?

（8）Sometimes as a housekeeper we have to go against traditions or policies to accomplish a goal. Describe a time when this has happened to you.

（9）The finest attention must be paid when preparing rooms. How do you make sure you meet the standards of the hotel?

（10）Tell me about a time when the work load was very heavy. How did you maintain production in our job as housekeeper?

（11）Have you set and reached your career goals as a housekeeper? How?

10.1.4 常用专业词汇

Vocabulary

turn-down service	夜床服务	make up	打扫房间
tidy up	稍稍整理	laundry items	洗衣项目
express service	加快服务	private room	包间
rent	租	adapter	连接器
brief ease	公文包	switch	开关
wardrobe	衣柜、衣橱	mattress	床垫
air-conditioner	空调器	thermos	热水瓶

第十章 申请客房部工作人员(How to Apply for Jobs in Housekeeping Department)

iron	熨烫	mend	修补
dry-cleaned	干洗	miscellaneous	杂物
compensation	赔偿	DND sign	请勿打扰牌
room reservation	客房预订	fully booked	客满
types of rooms	房间种类	double room	双人房
standard room	标准房	single room	单人间
suite	套房	king-size	特大号床
queen-size	大号床	twin beds	双床房
adjoining room	相邻房	service charge	服务费
extra charge	额外费用	full price	全价
discounted price	折扣价	rack rate	标准价
special price	优惠价	postpone	推迟
vacancy/vacant room	空房	cancel/cancellation	取消
book/reserve	预订		

10.2 英语情景对话(Dialogues)

10.2.1 Attend an Interview for a Housekeeper.

(Jean is talking with the Housekeeping Department Director Mr. Chen.)

Jean: May I come in?

Chen: Come in, please.

Jean: Nice to meet you, Mr. Chen.

Chen: Nice to see you, Jean. Your favored choice is housekeeper according to your resume. Can you tell me what previous experience do you have as a housekeeper?

Jean: Well, Mr. Chen. I've been working as a housekeeper in King Rose hotel for one and a half year.

Chen: One and a half year. So, can you interpret[1] the responsibilities of being a housekeeper in your perspective[2]?

Jean: Well, cleaning a set number of guest rooms each day to the standards required and carrying out guest requests such as extra beds, pillows, bathroom supplies are my primary[3] working responsibilities, what's more, reporting any damaged or missing items to the floor supervisor and completing deep cleaning projects as required are also on our working list.

Chen: Good. Jean. As you know, difficult customers are a part of any job in the hotel industry. As a hotel housekeeper you may meet these kinds of guests complaining about you when entering rooms or cleaning public areas. So how do you deal with situations like that?

Jean: Well, I generally handle unsatisfied customers by listening to them. The main thing a disgruntled customer wants is to be heard. So I let them speak first and thereafter I try to solve their problem. If the problem is out of my control then I will refer them to somebody like my supervisor or manager who can help.

Chen: Hmm, listening to what the customers are complaining about is very important. What are the most important skills required to become a good housekeeper?

Jean: I think a housekeeper should have the ability to work both individually and as part of a wider team and the knowledge of health and safety is also required when using cleaning chemicals.

Chen: You make a good point. Being a housekeeper should be strictly followed the specific cleanliness standards.

Jean: I couldn't agree with you more, Mr. Chen.

Chen: How long do you spend cleaning a room by the way?

Jean: Normally I take approximately 20 – 25 minutes for cleaning, refreshing the bathroom, making the bed and eliminating[4] trash of an occupied room.

Chen: Not bad. As you can see, the occupancy of our hotel is always stay at a very high rate, efficiency means a lot for our hotel, sometimes it's like crazy busy in our hotel, how can you manage to cope with that?

Jean: Mr. Chen. I love challenges, the more busier I am the more active and alert I will be while working, it makes me even more productive.

第十章 | 申请客房部工作人员(How to Apply for Jobs in Housekeeping Department)

Notes:

[1] interpret:解释,说明,诠释 例:We have to interpret his words in a modern light. (我们必须以现代的观点来解释他的话。)

[2] perspective:看法,观点 [U] [C] [(+on)] 例:View an issue from a historical perspective. (用历史的观点看待问题。)

[3] primary:基本的;本来的 例:The primary meaning of the word isn't used now, but you can look it up in a big dictionary. (这个字的本义现在不用了,但你可以在大字典里查到。)

[4] eliminating:排除,消除,消灭 [(+from)] 例:Alleviating and eliminating poverty remains a long-term historical task for china. (缓解和消除贫困仍然是中国今后一项长期的历史任务。)

10.2.2 Applying for an Housekeeping Manager

(Mr. Wang is being interviewed in the Personnel Manager's office for the job as the Housekeeping Manager.)

PM: Good afternoon, Mr. Wang.

Wang: Good afternoon.

PM: Sit down, please.

Wang: Thank you.

PM: As I understand you have applied to work in our hotel. Would you please introduce yourself?

Wang: I used to work as the Housekeeping Supervisor of Shanghai Pearl Hotel. Then I got a job in Shanghai Golden Palace. I am now working at the Housekeeping Department as a manager.

PM: How long have you worked there?

Wang: Three years.

PM: May I ask the reason why you want to work for us?

Wang: Frankly speaking, I'd like to join you because yours is much better than Golden Palace, and I have heard that yours is currently the hotel with the best training

& development policy, which is really a good chance for me to develop my career. I hope with my ability and the opportunity to work here.

PM: As an housekeeping manager, what do you think is the most important for the department?

Wang: Of course the housekeeping staff, which can be your biggest asset[1] or greatest liability depending on their dependability, attitude, experience, and work ethic[2]. They can largely make or break not only your success as a manager, but often the success of the department, and even the overall success of the hotel as well. Much of my typical day is spent working and interacting with them.

PM: Each manager must have a list of challenges, so how about yours?

Wang: In order to ensure an efficient and cost-effective cleaning operation, I really have a lot, such as dealing with budget cuts, hiring qualified people, retaining key employees, training employees, meeting increasing work demands, keeping customers happy, and communicating effectively with staff and customers.

PM: Which is the toughest challenge for you?

Wang: I think staffing is. You know much of the issue is tied to salaries and benefits, which I have little control over.

PM: What kinds of people do you have difficulties working with?

Wang: The only time I had difficulty was with people who were dishonest about work issues. I worked with one woman who was taking credit for[3] work that her team accomplished. I had an opportunity to talk with her one day and explained how she was affecting the morale[4]. She became very upset that others saw her that way, and said she was unaware of her behavior or the reactions of others. Her behavior changed after our talk. What I learned from that experience is that sometimes what we perceive about others is not always the case if we check it out.

PM: What are you expecting to make in terms of salary?

Wang: I'd appreciate it if you could make me an offer based on whatever you have budgeted for this position and we can go from there.

PM: Well. When can you begin to work here?

第十章 申请客房部工作人员(How to Apply for Jobs in Housekeeping Department)

Wang: I think, next week.

PM: Great. But before reporting on duty, you're subject to a medical check in the hospital. What about tomorrow morning, at 8 o'clock?

Wang: No problem. Where?

PM: In Wuhan Hospital. I'll have my secretary wait for you at the gate. By the way, would you please fill in this form?

Wang: Certainly.

Notes:

[1] asset: 财产,资产 例: The bank has assets of over five million pounds.(这家银行有五百万英镑以上的资产。)

[2] ethic: 伦理的,道德的 例: The beneficial combination of economy and ethic will lead to full-scale development.(经济和伦理的有益结合促进了全面的发展。)

[3] take credit for: 居功 例: I can't take credit for achievements made through collective work.(集体努力取得的成绩,我不能居功。)

[4] morale: 士气,斗志 例: The news was a boost to morale.(这个消息使士气大振。)

10.3 学以致用(Transference)

1. Listening. There are some sentences you will hear, and match the sentences to the pictures below.

A   B   C

国际酒店求职指南
The Guidance for Job Interview in Top Hotels

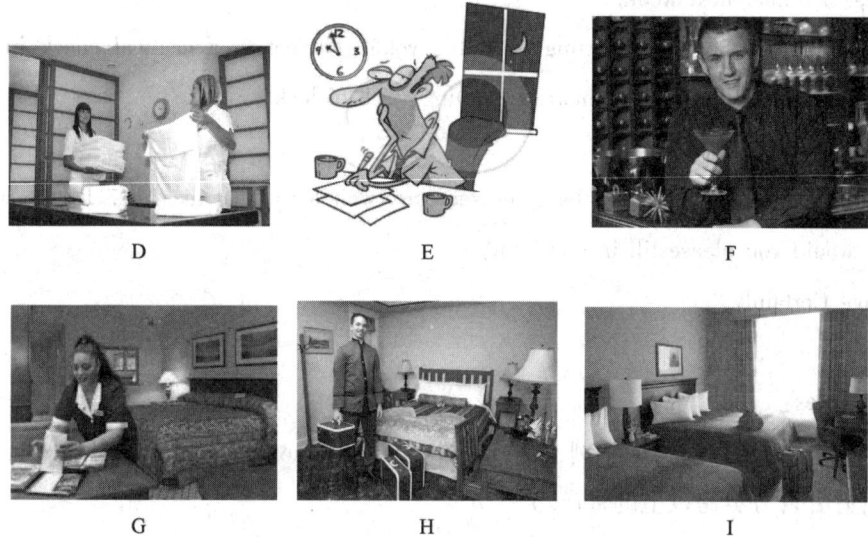

2. Read the text and pick up the proper responsibilities for the Assistant Director of Housekeeping.

   A. Inspect work to ensure proper standards of cleanliness and revise work schedules depending on the operation and occupancy.

   B. Supervise periodic cleaning tasks and ensure proper records are kept, inspect rooms and public areas and point out areas for improvement.

   C. Supervise the operational activities of the hotel front desk within hotel guidelines to provide the highest standard of courteous service while permitting acceptable profit levels.

   D. Recommend rooms that need spring cleaning or maintenance in coordination with Engineering and Front Office.

   E. Coordinate repairs and maintenance with Engineering and ensure that proper records are kept for rooms as in a Room History record.

   F. Determine discards of linen, towels, blankets and all other worn out items and recommend new purchases as when needed.

   G. Work with the kitchen and bar staffs on developing new menu selections and keeping the atmosphere upbeat and appealing to a diverse clientele.

第十章 申请客房部工作人员(How to Apply for Jobs in Housekeeping Department)

H. Ensure that uniforms are proper and order new uniforms as and when needed.

I. Keep an open channel of communication with subordinates and superiors on a daily basis.

Key Responsibilities of an Assistant Director of Housekeeping

We are currently seeking for who has the ability to deliver extraordinary levels of customer service and provide creative solutions to our guests.

As an Assistant Director of Housekeeping, she/he is responsible to assist the Director of Housekeeping in the daily operation of the Housekeeping Department and guide and develop a committed multicultural team to ensure the impeccable standards are met in all areas. The role involves bringing all the knowledge and standards required to maintain and surpass the guests' highest expectations and will include key responsibilities such as:

(1) _____

(2) _____

(3) _____

(4) _____

(5) _____

(6) _____

(7) _____

3. 请为下列岗位与其工作职责配对。

(1) laundry cleaner

(2) Room attendant

(3) Executive Housekeeper Management

A. Be responsible for department staff recruitment, establish and implement standard operation process for department, encourages the highest possible standard of environment management

B. Cleaning a set number of guest rooms each day to the standards required, reporting any damaged or missing items to the Floor Supervisor, carrying out guest requests such as extra beds, pillows, bathroom supplies and completing deep cleaning projects as required

C. Sorting, washing, drying, folding and pressing of laundry items using the equipment and machines provided and assisting in the delivery of hotel and guest laundry within the hotel

4. Complete the following dialogues.

Dialogue A

A: Hello, ABC Hotel, John Brown.

B: Hello, Mr. Brown, __(1)__ Li Min, calling for the interview.

A: Miss Li. Actually, I am waiting for you. I have known you very well from your cover letter and __(2)__ but I still have some questions. First… eh… Oh I'm sorry, could you wait a minute?

B: Certainly, please.

A: I'm really sorry to __(3)__.

B: You just said you had some questions to ask me.

A: But we really need someone who has __(4)__ in housekeeping.

B: I am quick at picking up things and I'm sure that I can fit for the position you advertised.

A: But do you know that we usually don't pay high to __(5)__?

B: I don't mind __(6)__. Since this will be my first job, I don't mind starting from a lower salary.

A: In that case, please come to our office at three this afternoon.

B: Then I'll come on time. Good-bye.

Dialogue B

A: Good morning. Sit down, please.

B: __(1)__. Thank you.

A: Welcome to the interview. Could you please tell me your name?

B: __(2)__. My name is Wang Dan.

第十章 | 申请客房部工作人员(How to Apply for Jobs in Housekeeping Department)

A: __(3)__ your resume, you want to be __(4)__. Do you have any experience with that?

B: I __(5)__ as a housekeeper in King Rose hotel for one and a half year.

A: Do you like the job?

B: __(6)__.

A: What about your English? Ours is an international hotel, therefore, we need our staff with __(7)__.

B: I pass the English Proficiency Test Band 6. This is my __(8)__. Besides, I won the second place in the schoolwide English Speech Contest.

A: That's fine. By the way, if you are hired, what salary do you expect?

B: To be frank, I don't know. But I am sure if __(9)__, you will be fair to me.

A: Well, thank you for coming, and we will inform you next Monday.

B: __(10)__. Good-bye.

5. Cloze

The Function of the Housekeeper

The job of a hotel housekeeper is to keep an assigned number of rooms clean. This includes a variety of services depending on the room's occupants. For a standard __(1)__ room, this will involve basic cleaning duties. For a room where the occupants have just checked out, the job is more difficult and involves __(2)__ nearly everything in the room. A check-out room must be so neat and clean that the new __(3)__ cannot tell that another family may have vacated the room only a few hours earlier. The housekeeper will provide fresh clean towels and toiletries and remove the trash, but otherwise leave the room alone. If a guest leaves a later service sign on the door, the room must be __(4)__, perhaps several times throughout the day until the sign is removed. One last __(5)__ is rooms that have been __(6)__ for several days. Though they have already been cleaned and turned over, these rooms must be revisited so the housekeeper can sweep and dust. By doing this, it can __(7)__ that the room doesn't look dusty and __(8)__ when new guests arrive.

(1) A. possessed   B. purchased   C. occupied   D. owned

(2) A. taking over　　　B. turning over　　　C. rolling over　　　D. crawling over

(3) A. housekeepers　　B. occupants　　　　C. employee　　　　D. staff

(4) A. checked　　　　B. revisited　　　　C. opened　　　　　D. closed

(5) A. consideration　　B. thought　　　　　C. method　　　　　D. idea

(6) A. purchased　　　B. vacant　　　　　C. full　　　　　　D. taken

(7) A. ensure　　　　B. provide　　　　　C. change　　　　　D. turn out

(8) A. beautiful　　　B. frustrated　　　　C. smart　　　　　D. abandoned

10.4　补充英语阅读(Reading)

1. 阅读短文并将下列选项与填入文中空白处。

   A. What job specific tasks did you perform in your previous organization?

   B. How much time do you take for cleaning an occupied room of a hotel?

   C. Why have you applied for this particular job?

2. 根据课文内容判断正(T)误(F)。

   (1) Well, housekeeping is the department or staff at a hotel or motel which is responsible for cleaning guest rooms and help with guests' registration process. (　　)

   (2) According to the test, when it comes to deal with unhappy guest, as a hotel staff, the first thing you should do is listening. (　　)

   (3) A good house keeper should possess good knowledge of proper usage and storage of cleaning chemicals. (　　)

   (4) Housekeeper is not a very promising position, so don't talk too much about the attributes of the organization that interest you most. (　　)

   (5) A successful housekeeper should be able to work in team as well as individual work environment. (　　)

   Before moving further into the article I would like to give a short introduction of housekeeping. Well, housekeeping is the department or staff at a hotel or motel which is

第十章 | 申请客房部工作人员（How to Apply for Jobs in Housekeeping Department）

responsible for cleaning guest rooms and public areas, changing linens, etc. Housekeeping is the work of a house keeper. Nowadays there is wide range of employment opportunities in this field. Below are list of questions which are frequently asked in interviews for this post.

Firstly, how would you handle a guest that is screaming at you?

It is very important for any hotel to satisfy their customer. Unfortunately unhappy customers are part and parcel[1] of running a hotel. Well, I generally handle unsatisfied customers by listening them. The main thing a disgruntled[2] customer wants is to be heard. So I let them speak first and thereafter I try to solve their problem.

Secondly, ___(1)___

Well, the answer to this question will differ from person to person. You can simply say that I take approximately 20 – 25 minutes for cleaning, refreshing the bathroom, making the bed and eliminating trash of an occupied room.

Thirdly, what skills are required to become a good housekeeper?

Cleanliness is one of the most important features a hotel. A good house keeper should possess good knowledge of proper usage and storage of cleaning chemicals. They must be able to handle all responsibilities in the absence of housekeeping manager. A successful housekeeper should be able to work in team as well as individual work environment.

Fourthly, ___(2)___

The follow is the sample answer: in my previous organization I was engaged in cleaning towels, linen, bedding, and workers uniforms. I used to wash, dry, and fold the laundry items. I even replaced soiled linen and towels, restocked soap, tissues, and drinking glasses, disinfected bathroom surfaces, dusted and polished the furniture, removed all trash, vacuumed the carpet and washed uncarpeted floors. I also replaced light bulbs, washed windows, drained ashtrays, and cleaned hallways and stairs.

Lastly, ___(3)___

The employer is looking for evidence that the job suits you, fits in with your general aptitudes[3], coincides[4] with your long-term goals and involves doing things you enjoy.

Make sure you have a good understanding of the role and the organization, and describe the attributes of the organization that interest you most.

Well, these are some of the frequently asked interview questions. Do not forget to say "thank you" to the person or people who interviewed you.

Notes:

[1] parcel:包裹　例:I sent the parcel express.(我用快件寄这包裹。)

[2] disgruntled:使不高兴的　例:Two countries emissary did not finish the job, disgruntled and return.(两国使者没有完成任务,快快而归。)

[3] aptitude:才能,天资　例:Edison had a great aptitude for inventing things.(爱迪生具有发明创造的卓越才能。)

[4] coincide:一致,吻合　例:My views do not coincide with theirs.(我的意见与他们不一致。)

附录 A

酒店部门中英文对照：

前厅部	Front Office Department
餐饮部	Food & Beverage Department
客房部	Housekeeping Department
销售部	Marketing Department
人力资源部	Human Resource Department
财务部	Financial Department
工程部	Engineering Department
保安部	Security Department

酒店职位中英文对照：

总经理	General Manager
副总经理	Vice General Manager
驻店经理	Resident Manager
人力资源总监	Human Resource Director
培训部经理	Training Manager
财务部总监	Financial Director
前厅部经理	Front Office Manager
值班经理(大堂副理)	Duty Manager
对客服务经理	Guest Service Manager
对客服务主任	Guest Service Officer
客户关系主任	Guest Relation Officer
前台接待	Receptionist

总机接线员	Operator
行李员	Bellman
门童	Doorman
餐饮部总监	Food & Beverage Director
行政总厨	Executive Chef
餐厅主管	Restaurant Supervisor
餐厅领班	Restaurant Captain
咨客	Hostess
餐饮部服务员	Waiter/Waitress
客房部总监	Housekeeping Director
楼层主管	Housekeeping Supervisor
公务区域主管	Public Area Supervisor
客房服务员	Housekeeper

附录 B

国际著名酒店集团标志

希尔顿酒店集团

希尔顿酒店

雅高酒店集团

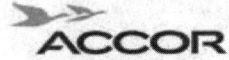

香格里拉酒店集团

香格里拉

万豪酒店集团

万豪酒店

洲际酒店集团

洲际酒店

喜达屋酒店集团

假日酒店集团

假日酒店

最佳西方酒店集团

最佳西方

君悦酒店集团

HYATT.

凯悦酒店

温德姆酒店集团

· 203 ·

参考文献

［1］王志玉. 品牌酒店英语面试培训教程. 北京:北京大学出版社,2011
［2］石定乐,等. 商务跨文化交际. 武汉:武汉大学出版社,2008
［3］Nick Stirk. 英语职场面试口语. 北京:外语教学与研究出版社,2010

责任编辑：郭珍宏

图书在版编目(CIP)数据

国际酒店求职指南：汉、英／孙嫘，王志毅主编
．－北京：旅游教育出版社，2014.3(2017.8 重印)
ISBN 978-7-5637-2566-3

Ⅰ．①国… Ⅱ．①孙…②王… Ⅲ．①饭店—职业选择—汉、英 Ⅳ．①F719.2②C913.2

中国版本图书馆 CIP 数据核字(2013)第 053774 号

国际酒店求职指南

孙嫘　王志毅　主编

出版单位	旅游教育出版社
地　　址	北京市朝阳区定福庄南里 1 号
邮　　编	100024
发行电话	(010)65778403 65728372 65767462(传真)
本社网址	www.tepcb.com
E-mail	tepfx@163.com
印刷单位	北京玺诚印务有限公司
经销单位	新华书店
开　　本	787 毫米×960 毫米　1/16
印　　张	13.75
字　　数	168 千字
版　　次	2014 年 3 月第 1 版
印　　次	2017 年 8 月第 2 次印刷
定　　价	29.00 元

(图书如有装订差错请与发行部联系)